MW01173661

LOVING
DISCOVERY

A MELODIC GUIDE TO RELATIONSHIPS, DATING, LOVE & INTIMACY WITH A PERSONAL TOUCH.

This book is dedicated to me. To my children. To my love.

To my parents. To my hopes and dreams.

To my past, present and future.

To you.

To the world.

To my beloved Bourbon and Boyshorts crew- Jeremy (my left-hand & Kyle (my right-hand) I am immensely grateful for the space you have created for me and my vision within your space. Your unwavering trust in me on this journey has meant the world. You have been a soft landing for my soul to speak its truth, and to share yours. Faith, vulnerability and laughter have carried us through. I am forever grateful for our bond and excited to continue changing the face of healthy love and happiness with your support. The true definition of "gentlemen" cheers to many more years!

To understand a thing, you must experience it.

May this book bring you all that you seek. May you find yourself, your love, and your beautiful future as you turn these pages...

I am a champion for love, now and forever. Dr. Tee

e·qua·nim·i·ty

/ˌekwəˈnimədē, ˌēkwəˈnimədē/ noun

mental calmness, composure, and evenness of temper, especially in a difficult situation.

"She accepted both the good and the bad with equanimity"

So much personal work is necessary before you can be anything to anyone. The problem is that we often become something to someone else before we find ourselves. So, what's the personal work that needs to be done?

Glad you asked…

TABLE OF CONTENT

Preface

After writing "Healing Discovery: A Soulful Guide to Healing When Therapy is Out of Reach," I realized the need to address a few aspects of being a lover. I started this book right before I started my PhD program in philosophy. I chose philosophy because it was more about knowledge, reality and existence which differs a bit from my collegiate psychology background. Philosophy "love of wisdom" is fitting for this time in my life. First, you are not what you do or what you have. Second, emotional control is key. Emotions are to flow through you, not remain stuck. Understanding the root causes of your suffering will change your understanding of life. Acknowledge, accept, and flow. All humans have and express emotions. How that occurs will always differ with each person. The suppression of said emotions is where the internal conflicts begin.

When many fall in love, they tend to think it will be forever. However, the realization that everything in life, including relationships, goes through different seasons and can bring about unexpected shifts. I had to learn these lessons as well. The outcome of these shifts depends on how we have learned to understand, process, and evolve from them. That is why we are here today!

While the healing book reflected some key points that I thought were helpful during my darkest days, this book is dedicated to becoming a better self-lover, parent and partner. As a Clinical Psychotherapist, I value the importance of reaching a destination, but as someone who deeply appreciates love, a lover's lover, I find joy in embracing the journey itself. While the destination may shift, a fulfilling journey provides me with the chance to truly explore and understand my own identity.

To foster more conversations around these themes, over ten years ago, I created my BTWNLVRS blog and recently a TikTok page for a wider audience. BTWNLVRS is dedicated to discussing self-love, healing, conflict, trauma recovery, and love for others; recognizing that matters of the heart are universal. Through these platforms, my aim is to bring a glimmer of light to those spaces that may feel dim and challenging.

I've been fortunate to experience different versions of love, although it hasn't been an easy journey. It has been filled with its own challenges, excitement, joy, deep sadness, passion, and life-altering experiences. As a divorcee, I feel blessed to have let go of anger, rage, aggravation, resentment, or bitterness towards my ex-husband, both in the marriage and its ending. It took a lot of hard work on my part. While I could provide numerous reasons to justify those negative feelings, the "why" doesn't matter when the "what" no longer exists. Expressing that would not change the outcome and I believe in forward movement. Initially, I was angry, scared and faced health issues like Printzmetal anginas is one word (Vasospastic angina), which required medical intervention. However, I eventually experienced a breakthrough and gained clarity. I began to work on myself on a deeper level. When entering marriage and starting a family, most people do not anticipate the possibility of the unit ending and becoming a single parent.

As a single parent myself, I have my daughters with me every day, except for alternating weekends and Sundays, which requires a lot of adjustments on my part with juggling home and work. It has been an incredible journey of self-discovery and resilience in the face of adversity. When unexpected challenges arise, it is crucial to prioritize nurturing our children's emotional well-being while also healing ourselves, as they did not have a say in this significant life change. Regularly checking in with them about the changes and how they are processed can be terrifying for them, especially if they are over the age of 5. They pay close attention to our moves and decisions as parents, as their young minds are in a constant state of learning and forming their belief systems. Therefore, I am mindful of how I make decisions and engage in deep conversations to include them. I actively ask questions and address any concerns they may have. I also involve them in some aspects of my life planning, as it is their life too. The changes I make have the most significant impact due to my time commitment to them, which has been a profound realization for me. By showing them my strength, I also demonstrate vulnerability by expressing my emotions and letting them know when I am overwhelmed and tired, so they understand that I am not a machine. It is important for me to teach them not to burn themselves out for anything or anyone and to avoid normalizing excessive strength, which can lead to stress and heart disease. We are products of what we see in the home, so I wanted to change the view. Instead, I am teaching them about the reciprocity of compassion and care and the importance of partnerships that involve helping one another in tasks to create a healthy balance.

When relationships end, it seems as if the ego tends to feel attacked and seems to hinder the heart from embracing the truth. My ego responded with a sense of audacity and entitlement, in response to audacity and privilege. But what is the truth? The truth is, I fell out of love with the pursuit of feeling loved and aiming to be enough.

I'm not one to give up easily, as I was loyal and stubborn. However, I acknowledge that this may not be the best combination for a healthy relationship. I believed in pouring myself into the dedication of marriage/familial bonds/friendships/home/children/career until I was empty, thinking that my then husband would refill me. But the reality is, people treat you the way you treat yourself, as we'll explore later. If I was pouring until empty, why would anyone want to deplete themselves in the same way, while watching the outcome? The clarity I gained from this experience is what I want to share with all of you. It is my heartfelt hope that you get to experience the epitome of love through my perspective. I felt compelled to write this to remind you that there is genuine hope, joy, love, and exhilaration available in the most abundant way possible. I simply ask that if you have chosen to pick up this book, that your mind remain open to giving love another chance and embrace the changes that may come from that decision. I will share playlists as I work on the chapters throughout the book. I chose jazz often because it allows me to feel the music while not hearing words. Music is stimulating to me, and I desire to shift my mind into the world of sound while clicking away with my heart and soul.

Introduction

First, let us set the scene. It is a quiet evening, and you are in the mood to relax but to also pour into yourself. Light a nice candle, turn on some music, grab a glass of something you love and cozy up in a chair or the bed. My favorite choices are Miles Davis, Coltrane, Jay-Z, Luther Vandross, Anita Baker, Thelonius Monk, Nat Adderley,

Light a nice candle, turn on some music, grab a glass of something you love and cozy up in a chair or the bed. A few favorites playing in my background are Miles Davis, Coltrane, Jay-Z, Luther Vandross, Anita Baker, Thelonius Monk, Nat Adderley, Kamasi Washington, Brandee Younger, Jasmine Myra, Kayla Waters, Theo Croaker, Vivaldi, or Joseph Bologne, Chevalier de Saint-Georges to name a few but there are plenty. There are multiple different genres throughout the book. I am currently listening to ChevalierSinfonie Liberté part 1 & 2 while sipping on some mineral water with a twist of lime. The lighting is a deep yellow on both sides of the room. The scent is teakwood, and the face is smiling. My heart is full. It is filled with love, passion, joy, excitement, gratitude, and a deep appreciation for the unknown.

You see, I am beyond my greatest known version of myself at this current moment. You are meeting me at my absolute best thus far, experiencing the version of someone who is in love and having the time of her life. I know how to love myself and others from a healthy attachment and high vibrational pattern. I have moved past the expectations and demands of my past, including those I placed on myself. You are experiencing the powerful, exuberant, outstanding, and defy-all-odds grown-ass Black woman!

A mom, divorcee, lover, fighter, healer, student of life and goal digger of dreams! My wish for you is to embrace your true potential as you delve into the pages of this book. Take a moment to gaze into the depths of your own eyes and affirm the love you have for yourself. Remind yourself that you are extraordinary, radiantly beautiful, and truly worthy of all the joys and opportunities that life has to offer. As we embark on this journey together, I want you to know that I hold you in the highest regard, for there is no force more transformative than love itself. Let us embark on this adventure with excitement and anticipation, for great things await us.

Sometimes, we jump into dating or relationships without fully addressing the wounds from our past experiences, which can have a detrimental impact on our current romantic life, partnerships, or marriages. However, by becoming aware of these patterns, cultivating self-love and self-awareness, embracing empathy and allowing ourselves time for introspection, we can enhance the journey and make it more enjoyable. Engaging in this healing process will create the emotional space needed to invite in more positive and fulfilling relationships. It may appear unlikely, but I encourage you to give it a chance and let's explore where this path takes us!

This book addresses some societal norms that are created by the social construct of gender roles and the expectations placed on individuals within a relationship. The Society is driven by the masculine versus feminine culture which has created such a divide. The goal is to break down these norms and expectations by creating a world that works for the beautiful human beings involved in them and cultivating relationships that are shaped by their own healthy choices.

This book is a loving guide, designed to help you become the best version of yourself as a lover. Opinions and experiences are interesting because everyone has them. These are my own, along with some simplified explanations of information and theories that we often hear but may not fully grasp. You may go to individual chapters for periodic insight but try a full read through first, to get a feel for the progression. It offers insights and practical thoughts to support you on this journey. Within its pages, you will find my personal reflections on love, passion, endearment, spirituality, and the idea of turning losses into victorious lessons. These reflections are compiled in the section titled "My Thoughts or My Reflections." It wasn't an easy decision, but that's precisely why I've decided to focus on vulnerability in this book. One particular chapter is dedicated to my own experiences, aptly titled "Rampage" due to its raw and unfiltered nature. Within its pages, you'll find a mix of emotions expressed through anger, joy, pain, and self-discovery. I've chosen to share this deeply personal journey because I want readers to know that I've been in the darkness before and have had to make these changes. Pain may be universal, but so is joy. Over the course of the past three years, I've poured my heart into these pages, deliberately leaving them unedited to preserve their authenticity. It was crucial for this book to remain true to its essence. As you read, you'll witness my tears, as they've been intertwined with the very words I've typed.

So, without further ado...

Chapter 1

HEALING FOR BETTER RELATIONSHIPS

Now Playing-

Musiq- Settle for My Love

Anthony Hamilton & Sunshine Anderson

Eric Benét- Femininity

Maxwell- Pretty Wings

Sometimes we need someone to simply say, "You matter." Here is your inspiration for the day: You matter, and you deserve to explore the version of yourself that may be hidden in the shadows. Avoid hiding from yourself. No one spends more time with you than you do. Allow yourself to uncover who you truly are and start sharing that with others. We are responsible for our individual energy and how it affects those around us. This can sometimes lead to anxiety and depressive symptoms in many people. Take a moment to acknowledge why you may be feeling that way. Address the emotions that arise, and if needed, allow yourself to cry and honor those emotions and the tears. Give yourself the moment to be soft and feel. Why are you feeling this way at this moment? What do you need right now? Where is your capacity at this moment?

Are you in a space to engage or do you need silence?

Learn to discover your true self, and you will find that your tolerance for unhealthy behaviors will change. This change will impact how you perceive the world and others in it. Your perspective on love, yourself, and the people you care about will also undergo a transformation. It is not the idea or dynamic of marriage, relationship, or friendship in and of itself that is the issue; it is the trauma within it. Becoming your best version creates better dynamics. We are the energy.

Self-love activity: Grab your favorite cup or glass that can hold at least ¾ of a cup. Keep a teaspoon next to it. This will be your physical cup of love. Instructions: place a teaspoon of water in the glass each day, speak your affirmation to your water and cover it. Each teaspoon is either a new or repetitive affirmation. Do this for fifteen days. At the end of the fifteen days, drink your water. You can do this while reading this book, "The Healing Discovery: A soulful guide to healing when therapy is out of reach" or when you just need an uplifting reset. This is your cup of love. Do not offer anything within that cup to anyone else because it may lead to resentment, bitterness, and anger. This will allow you to keep your cup full so you don't require others to do it for you.

You deserve to have the happiest, healthiest relationships in your life, and to do that, it's important to identify the patterns that might be holding you back. Do you believe you always attract the wrong types of people? Struggling with communication or trust issues? Maybe you've been hurt in the past and are scared to let your guard down.

Afraid to let your guard down with even the ones you love the most. Maybe you have never experienced healthy love, a healthy relationship or marriage. Or possibly what you have witnessed in your lifetime have been displays of unhealthy love dynamics which have created your idea of how to give love. Here are a few thoughts:

- It's important to take a step back and focus on inner work. This involves learning to become introspective and having trust and faith in yourself to become the best version of yourself. While you may not have met that version yet, it's crucial to create a safe space for it to flourish.

- Fear of failure often holds us back from reaching our greatest potential, but it's important to remember that trying is simply a learning experience, not a failure.

- Releasing fear of being alone. To discover the most amazing parts of yourself, it's necessary to explore and embrace solitude, even if it brings discomfort.

- Is it peace or avoidance? Reflect on whether you're truly living a peaceful life or if you're avoiding genuine experiences out of fear of challenges, conflicts, accountability, and change.

- Pay attention to repetitive behaviors and how they impact your pattern of attracting unhealthy relationships. It's important to normalize saying no to things you want to decline, even if you've previously said yes. Be your own advocate against relationship bullies, individuals who say they love you but continuously engage in actions that hurt you or disregard your boundaries. They may try to convince you that you're the problem, not them, by gaslighting you. They may also be in their trauma, but each person is responsible for their healing. Each day you have a chance and a choice, make decisions that suit the future you desire.

- Manipulative behaviors may have been present for months or even years. Possibly creating a conditioned response that makes them believe you're the problem because you failed to address it in the past or openly tolerated it. It's likely that you did have an issue with it, but you let it slide. The negative behaviors or things that are not in alignment with your relationship views that you tolerate in the beginning will possibly be the same reason the relationship ends.

- Additionally, jumping into a new relationship too soon can lead to similar issues. When you immediately enter a new relationship after a previous one, you may only focus on the actions that hurt you from your past partner. Failing to recover from that trauma causes you to share this unaddressed trauma with your new partner. Consequently, the new person only needs to avoid repeating the actions of your previous partner or do them on a lesser scale, leading you to believe they are your perfect match. This may make it difficult to see the person who they are because the focus is on them not being the ex. The lesser of the two evils isn't better, just different. This pattern occurs frequently and may prevent individuals from recognizing red flags because of making decisions based on their past trauma. They perceive opposite behavior as a sign of future success. Healing changes your vision.

Have you ever noticed patterns in others or yourself? Do you enjoy puzzles and games that challenge your mind? Identifying patterns is an essential tool for healing and transformation. By observing recurring themes in our behavior, emotions, and relationships, we gain valuable insights into our inner world. These insights empower us to consciously break unhealthy patterns and cultivate new, more beneficial ones. This process is liberating and empowering, enabling us to align our lives with our true desires and potential. The ability to create the life you truly want is an incredible feeling. Many people have relationship conflicts due to ego and lack of control in their childhood experiences and possibly other aspects of their lives. However, in this space, you become the co-creator of your most abundant life.

It may seem cliché but practicing self-love truly is another crucial aspect of healing and growth. Without loving and respecting ourselves, we cannot fully extend love and respect to others. Our perception of others is often limited by our perception of ourselves. Self-love goes beyond arrogance or selfishness; it is a deep appreciation and acceptance of our unique qualities, flaws, and worthiness. It involves recognizing our value as individuals and treating ourselves with kindness and compassion. It is the realization that people treat us how we treat ourselves. The more we love and accept ourselves, the better we can show up for the people in our lives. With self-love, we become more confident, resilient, and better equipped to handle challenging situations. It includes setting healthy boundaries, honoring our needs and values, and prioritizing our well-being. When we treat ourselves with kindness and compassion, we invite more abundance, beauty, and love into our lives. We begin to become our own greatest source of love and support. You begin to become your best lover.

Taking time to reflect is also vital for your emotional, mental, and spiritual health. This involves looking back on your past experiences, examining your emotions, and thought patterns, and identifying any areas that could benefit from a deep dive. It may be uncomfortable or even painful at times, but the outcome can be heavenly. By doing this work, you'll gain a greater sense of self-awareness, and you'll be better equipped to recognize when you're falling into old habits or unhealthy patterns. Oftentimes people change partners but attract the same traits as their last lover lesson (past partner). This will help you break that cycle and approach relationships from a healthier, more balanced place.

In the past, I would find myself staying in unhealthy or imbalanced friendships and relationships due to unhealthy attachment patterns from my childhood. But my daughters will forever be my greatest blessings because they taught me to love myself even before they knew their own names, and in turn, I discovered my true purpose. Their purpose is so immense that I had to come correct and healed before they reached adolescence, so they could fulfill their own purpose on a grander scale. It had to be challenging for me to feel the need for change deeply enough to make that change, instead of them inheriting my trauma. This ability alone grants me the opportunity to raise them with healthy love, balance, grace, mercy, clarity, understanding, and patience.

In our instantly gratified and distracted world, it's easy to get caught up in the noise and chaos and forget to pause and listen to our inner voice. Those red flags that people insist on turning green when the chemistry feels right. Reflection allows you to connect with your intuition, higher self, and divine guidance. It can help you gain clarity, forgiveness, and gratitude, and release stagnant emotions and thought patterns that may plague your heart. Whether you journal, meditate, walk in nature, or simply sit still and breathe, make reflection a regular part of your self-care routine.

By engaging in these practices and committing to your healing journey, you can clear your emotional space and open to more positive and fulfilling relationships. You deserve to have reciprocal people in your life who support, uplift, and inspire you. Ultimately, healing for better relationships is a process that requires patience, dedication, and a willingness to be vulnerable and nurturing to yourself first and then others. And the end result is worth it: happier, healthier, more fulfilling connections with the people who matter most. Keep shining your light, growing your love, and spreading your joy! Take the time to do the work, cultivate your self-love, and reflect on your experiences. You deserve the best, and with a little bit of effort and intention, you can create the relationships you truly desire. The world needs more of your loving and compassionate energy!

"My Reflections"

I recently had a profound realization while reflecting on the privilege of birthing my two beautiful daughters. It is a tremendous blessing that I deeply appreciate. I experienced miscarriages before both pregnancies, and with one of them, I almost lost my life due to excessive bleeding. Both of my daughters are what we call "rainbow babies," and this reaffirms the restorative power of the Divine. It gives and takes away.

When I think about my children, I realize that the gift was not simply in me having them, but in them choosing me. My oldest daughter gifted me with unfiltered love. I hated being vulnerable and shedding tears because it felt like a weakness. Being pregnant with her showed me a different world of vulnerability. While my youngest gifted me with strength to defeat a dragon. Of course, not a real dragon but she made me feel powerful. They became the catalyst for a significant transformation in my life. I had struggled with a need for control due to a lack of control in my own childhood. However, once I understood that my daughters had transmitted the gifts of safe love and true strength to make difficult decisions; everything changed.

Chapter 2

LET'S CHAT ABOUT ATTACHMENT

Multiple attachment styles are seen throughout relationship dynamics. High trauma impacts relationship dynamics in multiple ways. Having a better understanding of where and how relationship attachment develops can be associated with childhood.

Let's start by defining attachment styles in relationships. There are four main attachment styles: secure, anxious-preoccupied, dismissive-avoidant, and fearful-avoidant. You may see different names and more detailed descriptions for the style, but these are the basics. Secure attachment style is characterized by trust, open communication, and mutual commitment. Anxious-preoccupied individuals crave intimacy and attention and may feel insecure in relationships. Dismissive-avoidant individuals tend to distance themselves emotionally and become uncomfortable with too much closeness. Lastly, fearful-avoidant individuals may oscillate between anxious and avoidant behavior, struggling with fears of rejection and abandonment. The following breakdown is by no means exhaustive, but it will provide a little clarity into the attachment styles. This can create patterns that influence their behavior on a regular basis in all types of relationships.

So, how do these attachment styles develop from the start of a relationship? It starts with our early childhood experiences. The kind of attachment we develop with our primary caregivers shapes our attachment style in adult relationships.

1. Secure Attachment Style: People with a secure attachment style are confident, caring, and able to communicate their feelings effectively. They have a positive outlook on life and their relationships, and they are comfortable with emotional intimacy. Secure individuals are able to trust others, and they feel safe and secure in their relationships. A person with a secure attachment style in a relationship tends to feel comfortable with emotional intimacy and healthy communication. They can express their needs and opinions while simultaneously remaining open to their partner's.

    They feel secure in their relationships and are confident that their partner will be there for them when they need them. People with a secure attachment style tend to have healthy and long-lasting relationships with their partners.

    They are also typically able to establish healthy relationships early in life. This is often due to having caregivers who were consistently responsive to their needs, providing them with a sense of safety and trust. As adults, they tend to have confidence in their partners and are comfortable both relying on them when needed and being relied upon themselves. If this is not your attachment style, please try not to be too hard on yourself. It's important to remember that many people have had challenging childhoods that have influenced their attachment styles in unhealthy ways.

2. Anxious Attachment Style (Preoccupied): People with an anxious attachment style can be passionate and deeply emotional, but they also tend to be clingy, sensitive, and insecure. They often fear abandonment and seek constant reassurance from their partner. Anxious individuals struggle with communication and may struggle to effectively express their needs and desires. A person with an anxious attachment style in a relationship tends to be preoccupied with their partner's behaviors and the status of the relationship. They crave closeness and reassurance and may feel anxious or fearful if they feel their partner is pulling away. They often worry about their partner's fidelity and fear that their partner will leave them. At times, their anxiety and fear may manifest in overbearing or jealous behaviors in the relationship. People who develop an anxious attachment style often had caregivers who were inconsistent in their responsiveness. As a result, these individuals may have felt that they needed to be hypervigilant to ensure they received the necessary care and attention. In adult relationships, this can translate into anxious tendencies such as excessive worrying about the relationship, frequent or even irrational communication, and an intense desire for closeness.

3. Avoidant Attachment Style (Dismissive): People with an avoidant attachment style may come across as aloof, cool, or independent.

    They value autonomy and self-sufficiency and may be viewed as unemotional or detached. Individuals with an avoidant attachment style tend to have trouble forming close emotional bonds and may struggle with commitment. A person with an avoidant attachment style in a relationship tends to feel uncomfortable with emotional closeness or depending on others. They may have a difficult time fully trusting their partner and may feel overwhelmed by too much affection or intimacy. They tend to prioritize their independence and may become distant in the relationship to protect themselves from potential rejection or disappointment. This can make it difficult for them to form and maintain deep connections with their partner. Those with an avoidant attachment style may have had caregivers who were emotionally distant, neglectful, or rejecting. This can result in individuals who are apprehensive about forming close emotional bonds with others. As adults, those with an avoidant style may struggle with intimacy and may be reserved or distant in their interactions with partners. As a child they may have learned to suppress their emotions in childhood. This may be due to a caregiver that discouraged displays of vulnerability. The child then grows to be excessively independent and often keeps people at an emotional distance- hence their later behavior in relationships.

Fearful Attachment Style: A person with a fearful attachment style in a relationship tends to have a mix of anxious and avoidant behaviors. They struggle with wanting emotional closeness and needing space at the same time. They may fear abandonment, but also have a difficult time committing to a relationship because they fear being hurt or rejected. They may be indecisive at times, sending mixed signals to their partner which can create confusion and tension in the relationship.

4. Fearful-Avoidant Attachment Style or (Disorganized): People with a fearful-avoidant attachment style are pulled between their desire for intimacy and their fear of being hurt or abandoned. They may

desire closeness and independence simultaneously, and this can be confusing and overwhelming. Fearful-avoidant individuals struggle with trust and may feel anxious or avoidant in relationships. They also tend to have turbulent or chaotic childhood experiences. Caregivers may have been insensitive, emotionally abusive, or neglectful. As a result, disorganized individuals may have difficulty regulating their emotions and may have inconsistencies in their attachment behavior as adults. The caregiver could be overly indulgent, then distant and punitive at other times. This sporadic care could lead to attachment issues in adulthood, impacting how they show vulnerability in relationships.

Of course, everyone's experiences are unique, and their attachment styles can stem from a variety of factors, including grief in childhood. However, I hope that this overview of general attachment style development is helpful!

Overall, attachment styles can affect how we relate to others and shape our approach to intimacy and connection. Understanding and acknowledging our own attachment style can help us develop stronger, healthier relationships. It's important to recognize that attachment styles in relationships are not necessarily set in stone, they can change over time as we experience and process different situations and emotions in life. Knowing your own attachment style and working to communicate and compromise with your partner's attachment style can lead to a healthier and more fulfilling relationship for both parties.

My Thoughts:

This is a concise overview of attachment styles, but it is recommended that you conduct further research if you are unsure about which styles are impacting your life. It is common for individuals with unhealthy attachment styles to have unreasonable expectations of others. If you find it challenging to maintain relationships, consider using a guided journal or seeking therapy to engage in self-reflection, take accountability, and assume responsibility. It is easy to point fingers at others when relationships or friendships don't work out, but it is important to recognize that you are the common denominator. The goal is to experience love and respect from those around you while also being able to provide that for yourself, so you do not feel depleted with excessively high expectations of others. Do you tend to have high expectations of friends because your partner is unable to fulfill your needs in a healthy way? Do you overcompensate in every relationship you have? Are you typically anxious due to constantly ruminating about what you are not receiving from others? Unhealthy attachments will persist until you put in the necessary work. If they continue to exist, so will your patterns. Personally, I had experienced a phase of overcompensating in all my past relationships. Upon recognizing my own unhealthy attachment styles, I have set healthy boundaries and terminated friendships and relationships that demanded more from me than I could sustain. This was crucial for the preservation of my well-being and to cultivate a thriving life. The people who benefited from my lack of boundaries and unhealthy attachment style did not appreciate this change, but I do because it was necessary and I am my best self for me and my daughters. It has been incredibly healing for my personal growth. Once I made these changes, I started attracting everything I desire and deserve.

That time and those relationships were essential for my development and to understand my self-worth. The work is not easy and can be painful initially, but breaking down your own barriers is the first step towards building a new, strong, and healthy foundation.

Chapter 3

SUGGESTIONS TO BECOME MORE SECURELY ATTACHED.

** Here are a few suggestions on how to become more securely attached in your relationships:

1. Practice Self-Awareness: To become more securely attached, it's essential to increase your self-awareness. This may involve exploring your past experiences and any patterns in your behavior or relationships that may be impacting your ability to form secure relationships. Recognizing your strengths, weaknesses, and emotions and striving to foster a positive self-image is crucial. It is an image that you truly deserve, especially considering how heartbreak and heartache can often affect one's confidence. Identify and acknowledge any attachment issues or insecurities you may have. This means recognizing and admitting the past experiences or traumas that have led to your attachment style.

2. Cultivate Emotional Intelligence and solid communication: Developing emotional intelligence can also help to cultivate healthier, secure relationships. Being emotionally aware, effectively expressing your emotions, and showing empathy towards others can all help cultivate a secure attachment style. Many have spoken about the inability to express their emotions for various reasons.

Gaining a deep understanding of emotions and how they can be expressed in ways that may not be immediately apparent can bring clarity to any given situation. Communication is key when it comes to building secure relationships. It's important to be able to express your needs and wants, and to actively listen to your partner's needs and wants.

3. Learn About Your Partner: Take the time to learn more about your partner, their communication style, and their attachment style.

    Understanding them better can help you to create a more secure and trusting relationship. Consistently prioritize your relationship and make time for it. This includes spending quality time together, showing affection and appreciation, and demonstrating reliability and trustworthiness. Stay present and mindful in your relationship and avoid dwelling on the past or projecting fear onto the future. The present is not just being in the room, it's the essence and engagement.

4. Practice Vulnerability: Vulnerability is a critical part of building secure relationships. It involves being open, honest, and sharing your feelings and thoughts with your partner. Stepping outside of your comfort zone in this way can help to increase intimacy and strengthen the connection between you and your partner.

5. Practice Self-Care: It's important to practice self-care to maintain a healthy sense of self and build a positive relationship with yourself. This may involve engaging in activities that help you to feel centered and relaxed, like exercise, tai chi or meditation for your

emotional well-being. By taking care of yourself, you'll be better equipped to build and maintain secure relationships with others.

6. Strive for a balance between independence and interdependence in your relationship. This means pursuing your own hobbies and passions, while also fostering a close, supportive partnership with your significant other.

Overall, becoming more securely attached in relationships requires self-reflection, emotional vulnerability, and a willingness to work on oneself and one's partnership.

Thoughts & Feelings

Date & Time:

Song Choice:

Current Emotion:

Thoughts & Feelings

Date & Time:

Song Choice:

Current Emotion:

Chapter 4

ATTRACTING LOVE

Now Playing:

Quincy Jones- Moody's Mood for Love

Babyface- Exceptional

Rashaan Patterson- Sent from Heaven

It's important to have a clear understanding of what you're looking for in a partner. Once you have absorbed and begun to address the previous chapters, you may find that you attract more aligned people in your current energy. You will likely yield better results after you have done this work. Oftentimes people notice that they are attracted to a certain type but are unaware as to the reason. We have manifested everything we desire, even the things that aren't so great. People lie, energy does not. Even nice people can emit negative energy. The two ways this can occur are by focusing on the thing they are trying to avoid and if they are not forgiving of themselves. If you are afraid that you will never find a good man/woman, you won't. When your fears become your focus, you begin manifesting them. Not forgiving yourself can block your blessings because you don't feel deserving of them. You can't attract what you don't deserve. Clarity is key when dealing with people and it will make your life easier. This chapter will focus on how to manifest the love you desire by setting intentions, visualizing, and practicing gratitude. Additionally, we'll dive into the concept of energy and how it can affect what we attract into our lives.

Sometimes, individuals may find themselves unsure of their desires and their own identities. This uncertainty can make it challenging to navigate relationships, as genuine intentions can be called into question. It's essential to ask yourself a few key questions to determine if you are truly ready to date and be in a relationship:

1. Reflect on your motivations and societal pressures: Are you seeking to date simply for experience or societal and familial expectations? Do you genuinely desire a committed relationship or simply want them off the market? Pressures from age and even culture can be overwhelming. It's important to be honest with yourself about what you truly want and communicate this with potential partners. Don't be afraid to lose them, that transparency may be mutual, and you may both find a solution that works well.

2. Evaluate your readiness: Take a moment to assess if you are emotionally and mentally prepared for a relationship. Are you in a stable place in your life where you can invest time, money, energy, and emotional support into a partnership? Being self-aware about your readiness will help you avoid unnecessary heartache and ensure you can be a supportive partner.

3. Consider your expectations: Reflect on your expectations for a relationship. Are they realistic and healthy? It's crucial to have a clear understanding of what you are looking for in a partner and what you are willing to bring to the relationship. Open and honest

communication about expectations is vital for building a strong foundation.

4. Embrace self-discovery: Before entering a relationship, it's important to have a sense of self and a solid understanding of your own values, goals, and boundaries. Take the time to explore who you are and what you want from life. This self-discovery will not only enhance your own personal growth but also contribute to the success of any future relationship.

Remember, being ready for a relationship is a personal journey, and it's okay to take the time you need to fully understand yourself and your desires.

Everything in the universe is made up of energy, including our thoughts, emotions, and intentions. When we align our energy with love, we become a magnet for loving relationships. Understanding how to harness and direct our energy is key to manifesting the love we desire. By consciously raising our vibrational frequency through positive thoughts, self-love, and compassion, we create the perfect conditions for love to enter our lives.

Visualizing is a key component of manifesting love or anything for that matter. By vividly imagining ourselves in a loving and fulfilling relationship, we send a powerful message to the universe. Our thoughts and emotions create energetic vibrations that attract similar frequencies. So, as we visualize a love that brings us joy, we begin to align with that frequency, making it easier for love to find its way to us. Close your eyes and really feel it. What does it sound like? What does it look like?

Practicing gratitude is a game-changer when it comes to manifesting love. By expressing gratitude for the love we already have in our lives, we open up space for more love to flow in. Gratitude acts as a powerful magnet, attracting love and abundance. It also helps us cultivate a positive mindset, which is essential for manifesting our desires.

My Thoughts: Lovers Wisdom

It's completely understandable to feel scared and want to shield yourself from love due to past trauma. Many individuals shy away from relationships because they fear the vulnerability that comes with it. This vulnerability often forces people to confront and overcome communication and emotional barriers that may have been hidden due to childhood or past relational trauma.

However, it's important to recognize that embracing love and working through these barriers can lead to incredible self-discovery and personal growth. You may uncover aspects of yourself that make you an exceptional partner, attracting someone who is truly ideal for you. While no one is perfect, the energy that comes from this growth and self-love can feel like perfection.

These lessons and experiences can guide you towards a path where you deserve to be with someone who loves you in a healthy and fulfilling way. Sometimes, we have to go through challenges, struggles, and find joy in order to fully appreciate the blessings that come our way. These blessings can manifest within us and within a potential partner.

A partner can illuminate a side of you that you may have never experienced before. They can bring warmth to your coldest days and provide support during the darkest times. Opening your heart again and putting in the effort to understand and learn about them can be scary, but it's important to remember that they are also learning about you. They can witness and love this version of you, and just imagine how much more love you can experience when someone adds to that love in a healthy way.

By loving yourself and allowing someone to love you in a way that aligns with your understanding of healthy love, you are creating a beautiful foundation for a fulfilling relationship. Don't be afraid to teach them how to love you and to become a student of theirs as well.

Chapter 5

CREATING EMOTIONAL DIVERSIONS AND RELEASING NEGATIVITY

Now Playing- Vivaldi- The Four Seasons

It can be difficult to navigate emotions when emotional processing is not prioritized in many families. Try to pay attention to whether you are finding fault with the people who hurt you in your past to avoid facing yourself. This would be after you have worked through your previous traumas and are actively in forward movement. If you notice that you regress once you have processed your past, made great progress, and now focusing on yourself, sit back and explore that. When a person has been victimized, they may regress to that space when it is time for introspection and accountability. It is not always conscious, but the possibility exists because it can be frightening to make changes within self. The hardest changes may come from taking multiple losses due to not understanding this pattern and the personal damage that may have occurred.

Letting go of negative thoughts and emotions is essential when it comes to finding love. I know this has been said plenty of times before, but this is crucial. Holding on to past hurts and negative experiences can create a cloud of negativity that hinders our ability to attract and maintain a healthy relationship. By releasing these negative thoughts and emotions, we create space for love to enter our lives. Holding on to these patterns puts the control in the other person's hands. The person who controls the emotions, controls the mind. They control the mind, control the body. Allow your emotions to flow.

Self-sabotage can have such a deafening effect on a person. Notice whether avoiding emotional expression is occurring due to discomfort with being vulnerable. Lashing out when vulnerability tries to break through may indicate avoidance of discomfort and protection from potential trauma or the fear of it. Emotional vulnerability may cause feelings of anxiety and somatic symptoms such as shaking or fidgeting, sweating, feeling dizzy or multiple stomach issues. These symptoms may cause a person to want to flee or rage out to avoid further exacerbation.

What is being held onto that triggers this response? What causes the discomfort? When is this most apparent?

Managing stress, anxiety, and other negative feelings is key to letting go. One technique is practicing self-care, which involves engaging in activities that bring joy and relaxation. Whether it's taking a walk-in nature, practicing yoga, or indulging in a favorite hobby, self-care helps alleviate stress and promotes a positive mindset.

Surrounding ourselves with positive and supportive people can have a profound impact on our overall well-being. Building a network of individuals who uplift and encourage us creates an environment that fosters personal growth and emotional well-being. These positive connections provide a support system that helps us let go of negativity and embrace love.

Another technique to manage negative thoughts and emotions is through journaling. Writing down our thoughts and feelings allows us to gain clarity and perspective. It helps us identify patterns of negativity and provides an outlet for processing and releasing these emotions. Journaling can be a powerful tool for self-reflection and personal growth on the journey to finding love.

Practicing gratitude is also instrumental in letting go of negativity. By focusing on the positive aspects of our lives and expressing gratitude for them, we shift our attention away from negative thoughts and emotions. Gratitude helps us cultivate a mindset of abundance and attracts more positivity into our lives, including love.

People seemingly self-sabotage because they are used to things going wrong and people failing them. It's possibly a trauma response from childhood on up where the shoe kept falling around them, so it became the expectation. A good way to combat that is to start checking yourself. Talk yourself through it. Say things like "I recognize that I deserve better and desire more and in this moment, I am making things difficult. I am deserving of good things and will live in the moment as it is currently." Teaching yourself to reprogram your thinking will be helpful in your healing process.

Letting go of negative thoughts and emotions is vital for finding love. By managing stress, surrounding ourselves with positive people, practicing self-care, journaling, and cultivating gratitude, we create an environment that fosters personal growth and emotional well-being. This, in turn, opens the door for love to enter our lives and allows us to build healthy and fulfilling relationships.

My Reflections:

Relationship Lessons- The Twenty-Somethings Mindset

Now playing: Jay-Z Blueprint II

H.E.R- Gone Away

Raheem DeVaughn- Cry Baby

Kanye West- Good Morning

I remember being a young adult, possibly in my late teens or early twenties, and never really thinking about or wanting to get married. However, by my mid-twenties, I had been proposed to four times, with only one "yes" from my end. What made them want to propose, was it that I was loyal, catering, and ambitious? Was it me they wanted or what I did for them? It always made me wonder why so many women saw marriage as an achievement, while many men did not share the same perspective. It perplexed me that some women saw it as a milestone in their lives, as if it defined their womanhood. Society had ingrained in women the belief that their worth was tied to their ability to keep a man, while many men were taught that their worth was tied to their ability to provide financially.

It wasn't until I got married and observed the relationships around me, both past and present, that I began to gain a deeper understanding. I realized that the equal balance my parents had in maintaining our household was not the norm for many others, including myself. In our society, girls are often raised to learn how to serve, taking on tasks like cooking, cleaning, and caring for others. Unfortunately, Black women are often taught to settle for less and take on even more responsibilities. Being considered the "strong ones" without ever asking for the role. They are expected to be financially independent while also providing and caring for the family, as well as managing the household. On the other hand, many boys are not typically raised in the same manner. They are not taught the same skills of cooking, cleaning, and taking care of a home, nor are they educated about being a helpful partner in all aspects, including raising children. Of course, there are exceptions to this, as there are no absolutes in this matter. However, this information applies to a significant portion of men and women who come from similar backgrounds, influenced by societal norms for these groups.

Understanding a person's upbringing is crucial in understanding how they approach marriage or a relationship. It sheds light on how they value their partner, how they perceive the division of responsibilities in a household, and what roles their parents played in their upbringing and household duties. What did their moms and dads do in the home? How did they speak/treat one another and the children? It also shapes their understanding of what it truly means to be a spouse, partner, lover, and friend.

One significant difference I've observed is that some women value stability, whereas some men prioritize their emotions. These women may choose to remain in relationships, hoping to make them work for the sake of the family and children, while those men often leave based on their feelings and personal desires. The absence of affection or sexual intimacy can be a significant driving force for some individuals, though not for everyone. People often struggle to understand the various causes and effects that arise when their relationship lacks what they desire. It's important to consider the causes when observing the resulting effects or consequences.

I had numerous concerns and questions about marriage. It puzzled me why so many men would come home and immediately sit down to watch TV without checking if their partner needed help with dinner or taking care of the children. We've all witnessed grandfathers and fathers coming home and resting after a long day of work. But what about the grandmothers and mothers who also worked all day, picked up the kids, started dinner, helped with homework, managed bath time, read bedtime stories, and put the kids to bed, finally being able to shower and relax? This depiction has been portrayed on television for decades as well. Many of us love our mothers, and the first thing that comes to mind is, "I love my mom (grandmother), she sacrificed so much for me." Some men can acknowledge the sacrifices their mothers made but struggle to see the same level of sacrifice in their partners. Some may believe that their partners don't deserve better treatment than their mothers received. Others may solely focus on finances due to a poverty-stricken childhood, missing out on the full experience of the family they've created. Some of these behaviors may stem from unrecognized and unresolved trauma. The level of appreciation varies greatly. Sacrifice and exhaustion are closely associated with motherhood. Now, let's fast forward a bit and talk about today's society. Some men today want to know what their partner brings to the table. Now, if she brings equal pay or a well-paying job, contributes to paying bills, takes care of household chores, cares for the children, and even breastfeeds, could this question be irrelevant? I've heard men mention these requirements, and it's confusing if they aren't willing to bring the same things themselves. Let's say he helps her secure a better-paying job, improves her credit, and teaches her financial savvy. He also has a good-paying job, excellent credit, and maybe even owns a house or two. Does this mean he no longer needs to make romantic gestures, participate in household chores, contribute to raising the children, or reciprocate in ways that his partner understands? Many men I've spoken to view themselves as a catch solely because of their ability to earn and provide financially, but is that all it takes? These are just examples, but the point here is simple: the weight of the world cannot rest solely on one person's shoulders and expect the home to feel peaceful. You can reverse the roles as you see fit because no side is perfect, and we are all continuously learning. Communicate openly with your partner. Much of this can be missed when dating if the questions are not asked. Be open to learning how to be better because many people mistake avoidance for peace. They avoid doing the inner work out of fear of being hurt or repeating cycles. Cycles repeat lessons that were not learned. If times have changed, why hasn't that narrative?

Thoughts & Feelings

Date & Time:

Song Choice:

Current Emotion:

Date & Time:

Song Choice:

Current Emotion:

Chapter 6

RECOGNIZING RED FLAGS

Don't be blinded by who you expect a person to be or who you want them to be, see them for who they are. Truly loving someone entails accepting them for who they are in the present moment. When we focus on their potential to change or become someone different, we may unintentionally overlook their true essence. It is important to embrace the person in front of us, with all their strengths, flaws, and unique qualities, regardless of whether we agree with them or not. Allowing them the space to be their authentic version is a testament to genuine love and acceptance. With that said, it does not mean that who they are aligns with the partner you want or the future you desire and that is quite alright. This list of red flags is not meant to be comprehensive, but rather to draw your attention to a few important things. It can be challenging to address these issues when they involve someone you love or are deeply interested in. However, it's worth noting that what you tolerate in the early stages of a relationship often intensifies over time. Behaviors can become reinforced through conditioning, and our tolerance for negative behaviors can increase over time. That conditioning can lead a person to believe that their behavior is warranted due to the tolerance built through time. Set your standards early and have the necessary discussions.

1. When embarking on a new relationship, it is important to pay attention to the quality of communication between you and your

potential partner. Open and honest dialogue is the foundation of a healthy connection. In healthy relationships, it is important to have the freedom to express your thoughts and feelings, even when it comes to difficult topics. If you notice yourself constantly tiptoeing around sensitive subjects, it is worth exploring why that may be the case. Different childhood experiences can shape one's communication style, so initiating these discussions early on can help mitigate the potential for intense conflicts later. By addressing these matters openly and honestly, you can foster a relationship built on understanding and effective communication. However, if you notice a lack of active listening, dismissive responses, or constant interruptions, it may be a red flag indicating a potential breakdown in communication skills. By recognizing this early on, you can address the issue and work towards building a stronger and more understanding bond.

2. Honesty is a vital aspect of any relationship, as it fosters trust and authenticity. If you find yourself questioning the truthfulness of your partner's words or noticing inconsistencies in their stories, it is crucial to acknowledge these red flags. Avoid finger pointing and blaming and simply ask them directly. Dishonesty can erode the foundation of a relationship and lead to feelings of betrayal. By addressing these concerns openly and honestly, you can either work towards rebuilding trust or make an informed decision about the future of the relationship.

3. Respect is a fundamental component of a healthy and loving partnership. It involves valuing each other's boundaries, opinions, and feelings. If you experience a lack of respect from your partner,

such as dismissive behavior, belittling comments, loud tone, or a disregard for your needs, it is essential to recognize these red flags. Remember that you deserve to be treated with kindness and respect and reciprocate. By addressing these concerns early on, you can establish healthy boundaries and ensure that your relationship is built on a foundation of mutual respect. If you are not feeling respected, express your concern and make decisions based on the responses.

4. It is crucial to be aware of red flags in a relationship to protect yourself from potential harm. If you notice patterns of controlling behavior, such as excessive jealousy, possessiveness, aggression, gaslighting, manipulation or attempts to isolate you from loved ones, it is important to address these concerns. Recognizing these warning signs can help you avoid entering a toxic relationship where your autonomy and well-being may be compromised. Remember, you deserve to be in a relationship that supports your growth and happiness, and it is your responsibility to ensure that you are advocating for yourself. If this poses any danger to you, please reach out to trusted friends, family, or professionals who can provide support and guidance.

5. Emotional and physical abuse are serious red flags that should never be ignored. If you experience any form of abuse, such as verbal insults, threats, or physical harm, it is crucial to prioritize your safety and well-being. Reach out to trusted friends, family, or professionals who can provide support and guidance to aid you in the best next steps. Remember, you deserve to be in a relationship

that is built on love, kindness, and respect, and no one should ever make you feel unsafe or unworthy.

6. Lastly, it is important to remember that relationships are not guaranteed to last forever. This is in reference to all types of relationships including family and friends. While it can be painful to accept, it is crucial to recognize that both you and your partner have the right to walk away if the relationship is no longer fulfilling or healthy. By acknowledging this, you can approach relationships with a sense of self-worth and understand that your happiness and well-being should always be a priority. Remember, it is better to let go of a toxic relationship and create space for a healthier and more fulfilling connection in the future. At this stage in life, it is necessary to cleanse and clear what no longer serves you to receive what does.

A significant factor in all of this is the lack of accountability that some women often have towards some men. Those women fall into states of desperation due to societal expectations to have a partner that they are willing to accept men who have girlfriends, or even men who are married but claim to be unhappy. Some who have multiple children with different mothers fail to take care of the children. They may also be willing to be with a man who lacked vision and ambition with great sex but often complained about his shortcomings with no changes in behavior. As long as there are women who are willing to take in these men, tolerate their behavior, and remain silent about their responsibilities, it's no surprise that these men continue to behave this way. There are some men who are choosing women based solely on looks and body type, with no idea about who she is or what she believes, that has its own ramifications as well.

Again, reverse the roles as necessary because there are no perfect demographics and women have exhibited the same traits.

It's important to acknowledge that these issues are deeply rooted in systems of oppression, including both race and gender. However, it's also crucial to recognize that personal choice plays a significant role in these situations. Everyone has a responsibility to take personal accountability for their actions and choices in order for any meaningful change to occur.

My Reflections:

I have been through so much in the world of love. From feeling the love of parents, siblings, lovers, and friends, I have discovered something about myself. The lessons had to be deep for the reward to be abundant. Although I walk through the world with a smile on my face, my life hasn't been easy. Love and life have been such a great teacher. The tougher the lesson, the greater the reward, has been my story. I was breaking my own heart by making decisions fueled by my childhood trauma versus doing the work to heal. I wasn't even aware that I needed healing because I was such a lover of love and a helper of many. It was easier to help others, deflect or remain unaware. Healing taught me that I was using my love for people as a crutch, as many were using me and breaking me in the process. Not fully embracing my purpose and being deserving of what I desired for my life became my signature. I recall a conversation with my ex where he told me it wasn't his job to pour into me. I had always poured into him and anyone around me but that broke my heart a bit. I was a good person with a broken heart but wasn't aware because I hadn't done the work. I began the emotional and psychological heavy lifting and even shared my experiences with clients, so they understand what is possible for love on the other side of the healing journey. This love is the self-love that many speak of. It has by far been the most rewarding type of love I've experienced. It gave me the gift of looking back in my past to where my battered heart made the decisions that led to the broken heart. My energy started shifting once I began to visualize the present and future that I wanted. I started with binaural beats at night to shift my mindset from the daily ruminating. I began journaling, started, and completed EMDR trauma therapy which changed my life. I then began creating my "Manifesting Joy and Peace" journal (available on Amazon and my TikTok shop) and refocusing my energy. I used this journal to work on my manifestations versus a plain notebook. Going through my divorce felt more difficult than childbirth because I was birthing my new version. I didn't have the foresight to realize this during the transition, but it pressurized me until I imploded. That pain was the greatest gift given because it forced growth, faith, and forward movement. It taught me that when you really love yourself and another person, you are careful with their heart, thoughts, and soul. Many of us have been hurt by someone but please don't use that pain to determine your future. Please don't make the next person responsible for that pain and transfer that energy back and forth. People can only love you as far as they have loved themselves. When love is at play, it is so freeing, light, and beautiful.

Chapter 7

LEVELS TO DATING

Now Playing:

Whitney Houston- I wanna dance with somebody

Tamia- Please Protect My Heart

D'Angelo- Cruisin'

Dating must be the most frequently discussed topic I come across these days. It can take on many forms, and it's not always an easy process. Many individuals struggle to identify where they may be going wrong in their dating experiences. Some even view dating as a futile endeavor and prefer to remain single. Others engage in dating to alleviate loneliness without seeking a long-term commitment. However, setting the right tone from the beginning can help avoid the common obstacles that often arise during the dating process. This is particularly relevant in online dating, where a detailed profile allows for specificity. It is crucial to be mindful of what you are seeking, your intentions, and the energy you bring to the table. Are you genuinely ready for a relationship, or are you simply seeking temporary companionship? Many individuals have experienced the frustration of finding themselves on a date with someone they have no genuine interest in, simply because of feelings of loneliness or boredom. This often leads to complaints about the dating pool and wasted time. To address this, implementing a dating tier can be highly beneficial. The dating tier concept can be included in the "my thoughts" section, providing guidance on how to approach the initial months of dating to minimize wasted time, resources, and discomfort. It is important to communicate your intentions clearly, as the feelings, time, and resources of others should be taken into consideration. Additionally, it is vital to assess whether you would date and enter a relationship with your current self. Today's society has further complicated the dating landscape, with expectations from family, friends, and especially social media. While dating has always required openness and vulnerability, the influence of external factors has amplified the pressure and expectations associated with it. Ask yourself a few questions: What are the things that cause you to pause when dating? What challenges do you face and are they consistent with everyone? Are you showing authentically? Is the information you omit during the dating process something that will matter as time progresses?

1. When navigating the various stages of dating, from casual to exclusive, it is crucial to establish clear boundaries, standards, and expectations. Each phase of dating brings its own unique dynamics and complexities, making open and honest communication with your partner essential. By setting boundaries, you establish a shared understanding of what is acceptable and what is not, ensuring both parties are on the same page. This foundation of trust and respect is vital for a healthy relationship. If your standards or preferences change, it's important to speak up and communicate your feelings promptly. It is perfectly acceptable to change your mind, but it is not fair to keep your partner in the dark. Effective communication will foster continued relationship growth and development.

Additionally, it's important to consider that your partner may not be able to meet your needs due to their own limitations or capacity.

2. In any dating situation, being fully present in the moment is crucial. It's natural to feel excited about the future or dwell on past experiences, but true connection and personal growth occur when we wholeheartedly engage with the present. By directing our attention to the here and now, we gain a deeper understanding of our own emotions and desires, as well as those of our partner. This paves the way for more authentic and meaningful connections to blossom. Mindfulness, which we previously discussed in the "Healing Discovery" book, remains a key theme in this one as well. Being present goes beyond just being physically present; it involves actively engaging with the moment and the person in front of you. So, try your best to put your phone away, unless there are emergencies that require your attention.

3. Effective communication is key when it comes to expressing your needs and desires in a relationship. It's important to be open, honest, and compassionate when discussing your wants and expectations. By clearly communicating your needs, you give your partner the opportunity to understand and support you. Remember, effective communication is a two-way street, so it's equally important to actively listen and empathize with your partner's needs as well.

4. In the early stages of dating, it's natural to have some uncertainty and ambiguity. However, as the relationship progresses, it becomes crucial to have open conversations about exclusivity. It's important to discuss where both partners stand and whether they are ready to

commit to a more exclusive relationship. Learn what exclusivity means to all participants and ensure that each person understands. This conversation can help avoid misunderstandings and ensure that both individuals are on the same page.

5. Setting standards for yourself is essential in any dating scenario. It's important to know your worth and what you deserve in a relationship. By setting high standards, you are more likely to attract partners who align with your values and treat you with the respect and love you deserve. Pay attention to them having qualities that you admire. Avoid compromising on things you will find yourself complaining about later down the road. Remember, it's okay to have deal-breakers and to walk away from relationships that do not meet your standards. Try not to be upset if someone decides to walk away from you due to misalignment. It will save you both precious time to meet someone who is more aligned with your future vision.

6. Compassion plays a crucial role in navigating the different levels of dating. It is important to approach each interaction with kindness and understanding, both towards yourself and your partner. Dating can be a vulnerable and challenging experience, and showing compassion towards yourself and others can create a safe and supportive environment. This is especially true during this delicate time of dating, where people may not be accustomed to learning so much about a person. It can be unnerving for someone who hasn't been on the dating scene in a while, was not initially seeking a committed relationship, or never had to put much effort into attracting someone. Building personable and relatable connections

through meaningful conversations can be tricky if things have come easily in the past. By practicing compassion, you foster a healthy and nurturing dating experience for both individuals involved.

My Thoughts: The Dating Tiers

The truth is, there is no "set in stone" version of dating. This can vary from person to person, but it is simply a bit of a guideline to ease the stress of the dating world. Some individuals may progress through these tiers quickly, while others may take more time. Please, please have these conversations prior to advancing to the next step. Ask the questions and make your standards known up front. This is where you learn the person's capacity and standards to see if it falls in line with what you want for your life. It's essential to communicate openly and honestly with your partner to ensure that you are on the same page and comfortable with the pace of the relationship. If you choose to skip these steps, recognize that a lot can and will be missed and you can't go backwards.

Tier 1: The meetups- Casual Dating - This is the initial stage of dating where two individuals get to know each other in a more relaxed and casual manner. It typically involves going on casual dates, exploring common interests, and getting a sense of compatibility. Coffee, tea, quick grab spots such as Panera or Starbucks are great places to get to know one another briefly. These places are great for the first 5-7 meetups because you want to get a good feel for the person without the obligation of staying until the bill comes. It allows space to learn things about one another. Walks in the park, a trip to a playground, an arcade, or even bowling. Places were talking and a nice glimpse of their personality can shine through. This is more of the "lunch date "phase.

Tier 2: The Exclusive Dating - In this stage, the relationship becomes more serious and committed. Both individuals discuss and agree to date exclusively and focus their romantic attention on each other. This tier often involves deeper emotional connections, increased communication, and a sense of exclusivity. This is more of the "dinner date" phase. The intentionality of both individuals should be the same by this point. Dinner is more intimate, even down to the setting in the restaurant. The lighting changes, the music, and the candlelight. It sets the scene for a deeper, more intimate connection.

Tier 3: The Courtship/Relationship - At this stage, the couple has established a committed relationship. They have a mutual understanding of being in a partnership and are working towards building a future together. The discussions are more geared toward the planning phases. This tier involves a higher level of trust, shared goals, and increased emotional intimacy, strong communication, and a sense of exclusivity.

Tier 4: Long-term Partnership - This tier represents a deeper level of commitment and longevity. Couples in a long-term partnership have a strong foundation and are committed to supporting each other through the ups and downs of life. They may be considering marriage, starting a family, or making long-term plans together. This can be the final step or marriage may be. The last tier is simply dedicated to the commitment to one another.

Thoughts & Feelings

Date & Time:

Song Choice:

Current Emotion:

Date & Time:

Song Choice:

Current Emotion:

Chapter 8

LEVELS TO LOVE

Now playing:

Fantasia- Teach Me

Ledisi- Lose Control

Malia- Lucid Dreams

Destin Conrad: Cautious

Gerald Levart & Rude Boys- Written all over your face.

Ken Navarro- When we dance.

Jamie Fox- Light a candle

Love is a journey, and the type of love we experience can change over time. We'll look at different levels of love, from infatuation to deep connection. We'll discuss how to recognize the evolution of the love you have for your partner, and how to navigate the challenges that come with it.

Level 1: Infatuation - In the early stages of a relationship, it is common to feel a strong attraction and infatuation towards our partner. This level of love is often characterized by intense emotions and a constant desire to be in their presence. Some believe that the butterflies in the stomach are a reliable indicator of the infatuation phase, although it can also feel like an energy disruptor. However, everyone has their own opinion on this matter, and here is mine: it is important to pay attention to the person who brings you a sense of calm. The one who notices when you are uncomfortable and effortlessly puts you at ease. The one with the softness in their energy. Learn to trust your intuition on this one, but don't leave your brain behind. Signs exist for a reason, don't ignore them.

Level 2: Companionship and passionate love can hold the same level simply because either one can occur in level two of a relationship. As the relationship progresses, the initial infatuation may transform into a passionate love, which is more commonly observed. However, companionship before passion can enhance the bond between partners. This progression may be less common, but it provides different options without a right or wrong approach.

Companionship - This level is marked by a deep physical and emotional connection, a strong desire for intimacy, and a sense of excitement and adventure. Taking the time to really get to know one another increases the likelihood that each person will understand the other better. Spend time learning about each other and allow them to teach you who they are outside of a love interest. Late-night phone calls, falling asleep on the phone, giggling like school kids, laughing, crying, and simply enjoying one another while being your authentic selves.

Passionate Love - Over time, the love between partners can evolve into intimacy. This level is characterized by a strong bond, shared values, intense longing for one another, and a sense of comfort and security in each other's presence. Passion can sometimes fluctuate, running hot and cold, so having companionship first may decrease tension in those moments. This level is alluring, captivating, and deeply fulfilling. It is important to stay grounded and in touch with your life's desires while navigating this passionate love.

By acknowledging the importance of both companionship and passionate love, and understanding that they can occur in different sequences, we can appreciate the unique dynamics of each relationship. Embrace the journey and let your heart guide you as you explore the depths of love and connection.

Level 4: Unconditional Love - True love transcends flaws and imperfections. Unconditional love is a level where we accept our partner wholeheartedly, flaws and all. It is a love that is forgiving, supportive, and understanding, even in the face of challenges. However, many people find it difficult to achieve this level of love, often because they place conditions on their love. This is understandable, as many have experienced hurt in the past. It is important to recognize that love cannot be controlled, actions, yes but not love. The misconception that it can be leads to misunderstandings and restrictions. It is crucial to understand that unconditional love does not mean unconditional tolerance. If that attachment becomes unhealthy, it is important to pay attention to the signs early on. Releasing someone is also a sign of unconditional love. Loving them enough to know when the season has ended, while still caring for them. Knowing when someone is not what you need, but trying to change them, isn't loving them. There may be someone who truly loves them for who they are.

Level 5: Emotional Intimacy - Emotional intimacy is a level of love where partners feel safe to express their deepest thoughts, fears, and desires. It involves vulnerability, trust, and a deep understanding of one another's emotions. This level of connection can truly transform a relationship for the better. When both individuals show up with a sense of emotional safety, it creates a soft landing for each other. It is important not to take this soft landing or safe space for granted. Cherish and nurture the emotional intimacy that allows for open and honest communication.

Level 6: Intellectual Connection - Beyond physical and emotional intimacy, an intellectual connection is a level of love where partners stimulate each other intellectually. It involves engaging conversations, shared interests, and a mutual respect for each other's intellect. This aspect of a relationship can be incredibly attractive, particularly for those who have a passion for learning. You may find yourself drawn to individuals who possess a wealth of knowledge, have a keen interest in politics, excel in a particular subject, or are avid readers. The intellectual connection adds an extra layer of depth and excitement to the relationship, making it even more fulfilling and enjoyable.

Level 7: Spiritual Connection - A spiritual connection is a level of love that transcends the physical and emotional realm. It involves a shared sense of purpose, values, and a deep connection on a soulful level. If you have ever experienced a spiritual connection, you understand the profound impact it can have. It feels as if it was divinely orchestrated, with the other person truly understanding you on a different level. Synchronicities abound, and both parties are aware of them. Simple details become meaningful commonalities that seem almost too perfect to be real. This bond awakens a sense of gratitude for their presence in your life, and for the ability to attract them through self-love and healing. The spiritual connection is a beautiful reminder of the power of love and the interconnectedness of souls.

Level 8: Deep Connection - The highest level of love is a profound connection that encompasses all the previous levels. It is a love that is rooted in trust, respect, effective communication, and a genuine desire to witness each other's personal growth and success. This love endures the trials of time and continues to evolve and strengthen. It goes beyond mere presence, but rather embodies true and intentional presence. The gift of a deep relational bond is truly unparalleled.

In order to navigate the challenges and maintain a healthy balance between individual needs and the needs of the relationship, it is crucial at every level of love to engage in open and honest communication, practice compromise, and demonstrate a willingness to grow both individually and as a couple. This ongoing commitment to personal and relational growth is essential for sustaining a fulfilling and balanced connection.

Chapter 9

TAKING NEXT STEPS

Every relationship is unique, and moving forward requires different steps for different couples. When it comes to discussing long-term goals, it's crucial for couples to have open and honest conversations about their individual aspirations and how they align with each other's. This involves exploring topics such as career ambitions, family planning, and personal growth. By understanding each other's long-term goals, couples can work together to create a shared vision for their future and make decisions that support their collective dreams.

Taking a relationship to the next level requires a deep level of trust and commitment. It may involve milestones such as moving in together, getting engaged, or even getting married. These steps should be taken when both partners feel ready and have a solid foundation of love and understanding. It's important to have open discussions about expectations, timelines, and any concerns that may arise during this transition, ensuring that both individuals are on the same page and comfortable with the progression of the relationship.

Blending families can be a complex and delicate process, particularly when young children are involved. It necessitates open communication, patience, and a deep understanding of each family member's needs and emotions. It is important to ensure that you have followed the steps to help determine the appropriate timing for introducing the children. While nothing is guaranteed, if you have successfully navigated the major stages and are moving towards a more long-term situation, it may be time to meet the children according to your agreed-upon timeline and meet the co-parents if that is part of your arrangement.

Couples should take the necessary time to build relationships with each other's children, foster a sense of unity, and establish clear boundaries and expectations. By creating a supportive and inclusive environment, couples can navigate the complexities of decision-making and strengthen their bond as they face life's challenges together.

Chapter 10

BEING SUPPORTIVE

Partnership means supporting each other through good times and bad. In this chapter, we'll discuss how to be a source of encouragement and motivation for your loved one. We'll talk about ways to be there for your partner during difficult times, how to communicate effectively, and how to express appreciation.

Conflicts will occur but they usually arise when someone is trying to force the other person to their side. Conflict is healthy and can aid in learning to release control over the other person. Learn to manage conflict so you will be better at navigating these challenges as they arise.

Being a supportive partner means being there for your loved one during both the good times and the bad. It's important to create a safe space where your partner feels comfortable sharing their struggles and vulnerabilities. By actively listening and offering empathy, you can provide the support they need to navigate difficult times. Remember, being a source of encouragement and motivation doesn't mean fixing their problems, but rather being a steady presence and showing them that they are not alone. They must still do their own processing and self-work.

When your partner is going through a tough time, it's essential to be patient and understanding. Allow them to express their emotions without judgment or criticism. Offer a listening ear and validate their feelings.

Sometimes, all they need is someone to lean on and to know that you are there for them. Find out if they need a listening ear or a potential solution. By being a compassionate and supportive presence, you can help your partner navigate their challenges with greater strength and resilience.

Effective communication is key to being a supportive partner. It involves actively listening, understanding your partner's perspective, and expressing your own thoughts and feelings in a respectful manner. By practicing open and honest communication, you can create a safe and trusting environment where both partners feel comfortable sharing their thoughts, concerns, and needs. This allows you to better understand each other and find solutions together.

Expressing appreciation for your partner's efforts and qualities is an important aspect of being supportive. Recognize and acknowledge their strengths, achievements, and the positive impact they have on your life. Small gestures of gratitude, such as a heartfelt thank you or a surprise token of appreciation, can go a long way in strengthening your bond and making your partner feel valued and loved.

Have you ever noticed that sometimes, one person may only see the consequences of their actions without recognizing the behaviors that led to those outcomes? That good ole' cause and effect. It can be easier to focus on what we feel we are not receiving rather than acknowledging the impact our own actions have had to lead to the undesired effect. Every action has a cause, and it is unlikely for someone to respond in a certain way without a reason. In many relationships, one person may only see the effects without realizing that their own behavior is the underlying cause. In such situations, it is crucial to approach the matter with empathy and patience. Recognizing fault within ourselves can be challenging, but if a particular effect consistently occurs, there is likely a reason behind it. Encouraging open and honest communication with your partner can provide insight into their actions and their impact on the relationship. By fostering understanding and promoting self-reflection, you can work together to address the root causes and bring about positive change. Taking the time to reflect on your own actions and considering how you would respond if faced with them can be a helpful exercise.

Chapter 11

GROWING IN LOVE AND INTIMACY

Now Playing:

Anita Baker- Whatever it Takes.

Luther Vandross- Greater Love

Usher- Love you Gently.

Goapele- Cool Breeze

Maxwell- Sumthin' Sumthin'

    Healthy relationships require effort and attention from both partners. Relationships require effort and as time progresses, one should not decrease in effort and care. Don't assume that your mate knows you're still interested in them due to longevity. While constant reassurance isn't necessary, assurance may be. Continuously learn about your partner throughout your relationship. Don't assume that just because you've been together for years, that you still know one another. People change like seasons, and we must learn and adapt alongside them. Life happens, and time passes, often turning us into two ships passing in the night. Love may still be there, but the passion and desire may fade. The idea that the grass is greener elsewhere could be remedied by learning about the person you are in a relationship with. Try dating again. Make the time to meet each other at a location and pretend to not know the other. Engage in conversations about your current alignment and desires. Create a date-night bucket list, and actively knock things off the list. Be more intentional with daily touch and truly consider how you and your person feel loved in this current time and space. Place the same effort you would put into a new option, into your current person. Grass is green, where it's watered, not trampled on or covered in toxicity.

These are the moments when you can truly discover who your partner has become over the last few months or years in many cases.

It's about intentionally being in love, not just "falling" in love. Consistently expressing gratitude is incredibly important. It goes beyond simply saying "thank you" excessively, but rather involves truly valuing the other person and recognizing the value they bring to the relationship. It's easy to fall into the trap of expecting certain things from your partner, which can lead to bitterness or resentment if not reciprocated. Therefore, it's crucial to pay attention to reciprocity. Understand that expressing love and receiving love may differ from person to person. Take note of how your partner shows love and try to reciprocate in the same way.

Sit down together and establish a set of standards for your relationship. Remember, you have the power to start fresh at any point because it's your relationship. Starting anew involves discussing any issues, practicing forgiveness, and clearing the energy. Once these steps are taken, both parties can agree to approach the relationship with fresh perspectives, boundaries, and standards. It's also beneficial to periodically reassess your relationship as time goes on, like an annual check-up. This allows you to gauge if you're still in alignment and if you've both grown from the lessons learned in the past year. You can even choose your anniversary date or the halfway mark as a time to evaluate your bond, refocus your attention on one another and determine what actions are necessary to strengthen it further, if needed.

My Reflections: Take the time to sit with your partner and plan nights where you have a meal at home, on the floor with candles and music, and engage in conversations that help you get to know each other again. Investing in your relationship is not only beautiful, but also so sexy and fulfilling. You'll create a safe and happy space for both of you to thrive.

Thoughts & Feelings

Date & Time:

Song Choice:

Current Emotion:

Date & Time:

Song Choice:

Current Emotion:

Final Chapter:

RAMPAGE- UNCONTROLLED MIND AND EMOTIONS....

Now Playing:

Jazmine Sullivan- Reality Show

Toni Braxton/Babyface- Love, Marriage & Divorce

Jay Z- 4:44

Beyonce: Lemonade

Fred Hammond- Jesus Be a Fence

Jennifer Hudson- Moan

Anthony Ramos- Cry Today, Smile Tomorrow

<u>Well, hello there!</u>

As we dig into the pages moving forward, please remember this... there is a time in your life for everything you're experiencing.

The good, the bad, the joy, the pain and the indifferent are all a part of your divine design.

The current year is 2023 and this part of the book is not written in real time. I want to remind you that this book will have some chapters with active journal pages, as this may be your journey as well. What makes this book unique are the blank pages scattered throughout, meant for deep thought and reflection. I would love to hear a bit about you in your journey.

It is the year 2021, we find ourselves grappling with the COVID-19 pandemic. And you know what else? I'm about to embark on my final year in my third decade. With any luck, come May of this year, I'll be celebrating my 39th birthday. As a Taurus baby and a Venus sign, I possess a grounded and intimate soul. The past decade has brought me a plethora of experiences. Love and pain, motherhood and success, depression and financial literacy, anxiety and fear, knowledge and growth, happiness and joy. It's been a decade of graduations, businesses, and hope. But it's also been a decade of self-discovery, self-acceptance, and self-love. Peace and balance has found its way into my life.

During this time, I've grown mentally, emotionally, spiritually, and sensually. Oh, the sexual growth that has unfolded over these years is truly surreal and well-deserved. In my twenties, I was often confused about love, intimacy, and even convinced that I didn't derive much pleasure from sex (boy, was I wrong! But more on that later). My emotions were deeply intertwined with my sensuality. My self-esteem and confidence were lacking, and I realized that much of what I knew about these matters was shaped by the guys I dated. I was lost, like a child navigating an adult world. However, in this decade, I've discovered myself. I'm still learning, and whew chile... the journey has been something else! The intimacy and passion I've found within myself are truly captivating. I've developed a stronger sense of self and a deeper understanding of life. This decade has taught me about womanhood, about manifesting the life I desire, need, want, and deserve. Most importantly, it has taught me about myself. So, has your journey begun?

The Journey

Around the age of 33, I experienced a profound transformation that I couldn't ignore. It became clear to me that I needed to make a difficult decision: to request a divorce or take a break from my marriage. The pain had become overwhelming, and I wanted to give it time to see if there was any chance of salvaging the relationship. However, it felt like the trauma outweighed the love. Sometimes people cannot love because previous loss is too deeply rooted in the soul. This process was like an awakening, but I wasn't quite ready to fully move forward. That shift didn't happen until a few years later.

During this time, my spiritual journey accelerated, and I found peace through the passing of both of my grandmothers that year. They were both a force to be reckoned with. Hard working women who had too much on their backs to bare. It was interesting to watch such strength but also such pain. Being strong but in pain became the norm with our women. The weight of the world has rested on the shoulders of the women in my family for generations.

I must admit, I had a closer relationship with one grandmother, while the other was more distant. The closer one was like my soul, my spirit animal, my love. She was like a warm blanket on a cold night, bringing me serenity. We were connected on a deep level, and I always felt her love. In a way, she reflected myself, and I was a reflection of her. She truly knew me and saw me for who I was. I thought I had more time. We always think we have more time, but we are borrowing each minute, each day. Time is the currency we never earn back, spend it wisely.

I had the opportunity to visit my grandmother on a Saturday. It was a lovely visit filled with kisses, hugs, and even some muffins she had bought from Sam's Club. She insisted on giving them to me, saying, "It's my money, I'll spend it how I want." I couldn't argue with that, so I gratefully accepted the muffins. We made plans for me to return on Monday to help her with a phone issue. However, a rainstorm on Monday led me to reschedule my visit for Tuesday.

Little did I know that Tuesday would be a life-changing day. Just before heading to her house, I received a call from the fire department. My grandmother had suffered a stroke. Everything moved at a rapid pace from that moment on. She now resides in my heart, in the very air I breathe, and in my soul. I dream of her and feel her peaceful presence. She feels closer to me, and I find solace in that.

My grandmother had a deep love for plants. I, on the other hand, tend to unintentionally kill every plant I come across, even cacti. But there's a beautiful plant sitting in my bedroom window that's thriving like a champion. I named her Ivy, and I believe it's my grandmother's spirit that shines through her. Sometimes, I close my eyes and listen to the Fred Hammond version of "Jesus be a fence," a song my grandmother loved. As I write this, I hear the gospel song "I know I've been changed." It brings me a sense of comfort and connection to her. In this moment, my soul is at peace, my spirit is calm, and my heart is full. What fills your heart and soul?

The Lessons

Now Playing:

Whitney Houston

I Didn't Know My Own Strength

Why Does it Hurt So bad.

Try It on My Own

- I learned that in the past, I struggled to understand emotional expression due to my tendency to avoid it. My softness wasn't respected so the only emotion that appeared to keep me protected was anger. That excessive softness was tied to my unhealthy attachments and codependency from trauma. However, I eventually learned the significance of releasing other emotions. One emotion that I often overlooked and took for granted was sadness. It is important to acknowledge and allow yourself to experience sadness, as it creates a space for necessary processing and can ultimately lead to feelings of relief and joy. By denying sadness and avoiding the full process, you may hinder your emotional growth and potentially develop bitterness and resentment. With this newfound understanding, I then had to focus on learning how to control and truly comprehend my emotions.

Compassion and discernment became my balance. As a facilitator of healing, I often find myself experiencing emotions on a deeper level than maybe the average person. I am an empath, and as an earth sign, I am constantly learning to ground myself. However, I must admit that grounding can sometimes be a painful process.

Throughout my journey, I have gained valuable insights into love, loss, setting boundaries, and making mistakes. In fact, I found myself repeating those missteps for quite some time before truly learning my lessons.

One hard truth I had to confront was that I am a victim of addiction. It was a difficult realization to come to terms with. I discovered that my love addiction stemmed from deep-rooted feelings of abandonment and rejection that originated from my childhood. Understanding this helped me see how my love addiction led to irrational feelings of desperation and unhealthy attachments.

- I learned that sexuality and intimacy can be deep rooted in pain and suffering and will attract that. That energy exchange can and did cause depletion and the inability to fully heal. Taking on other people's demons while feeding my own.

- I learned how much trauma not only shaped who I was but created the inability to even see that a problem existed. I became conditioned to pain and I didn't even realize it. I became numb and expected heart ache, heartbreak. Felt normal, not good, just normal. I confused pain and chaos with love and the true form of love became unrecognizable. Love is not pain, not chaos, not confusion. Love is kind, warm and patient. Love is mercy and grace.

- I learned what it really looks like to OWN. MY. SHIT…. and unpack it. To have patience with myself and grow from it. To have mercy on my soul and forgive myself.

- I learned accountability and responsibility which helped with my emotional regulation, forgiveness, apologies, and comfort with vulnerability. Always a work in progress, both teacher and student.

- I learned that I didn't fully express the dark areas of myself out of fear of judgment, shame, or further abandonment.

- I learned that I had never been myself because it never truly felt safe. I had to be who was most accepted with no pushback. Pushback could cause people to leave my life and remember… I had abandonment issues.

- I learned that those dark areas are part of my story and to allow them to be just that, with only progress moving forward.

- I learned that control and possession do not belong in the conversation with real love and acceptance. What and who are divinely sent for you are for you. Some people are seasons of growth and not a lifetime of love. To release control meant to free my soul.

Have you begun to free your soul?

Energy source

Now Playing:

Duke Ellington & John Coltrane- In a Sentimental Mood

John Coltrane- Naima

After the Rain

I Love You

Miles Davis- It's Only Paper Moon

I was giving away my light, my energy and expecting others to replenish it. I had no idea what it meant to restore myself. *My* energy, *My* light. I thought that you treat people how you want to be treated and reciprocation would follow. Interesting lesson I learned; I will expound further in a moment. I find myself in a unique space where my energy allows only freedom, autonomy, and love. For a long time, I felt trapped in a state of confusion that left me uncertain, suffocated, and clinging irrationally. This stemmed from the hurt, fear, pain, and trauma I had experienced.

At times, my life was filled with expectations and the constant need to fulfill other people's needs. In those moments, I yearned to be needed, but deep down, all I truly desired was to be appreciated and considered. I simply longed for someone to be genuinely kind, without any pretense or expectations.

One of the greatest lessons I have learned in this decade is that people don't treat you based on how you treat them; they treat you based on how you treat yourself. I realized that I wasn't loving, kind, gentle, or forgiving with myself. My self-love was conditional, and I was unforgiving of my own shortcomings. I was slowly disappearing before my own eyes, and it became clear that the only person who could save me was myself.

Do you need a parachute?

Thoughts & Feelings

Date & Time:

Song Choice:

Current Emotion:

I can breathe again.

The true value of breathing is often underestimated until it is taken away. On April 2nd, 2021, I initially thought I was experiencing indigestion. I tried various remedies such as ginger tea, rolaids, and mineral water to try to belch, hoping for relief. Unfortunately, nothing seemed to work. As I bent over to tie my shoes, I even thought I heard water in my chest, which seemed absurd. However, with my breathing becoming increasingly shallow and the persistent chest pain, I decided it was best to seek medical attention.

An hour later, in the emergency room, I received the shocking news that I had spontaneous pneumothorax. A chest tube was painfully placed in the ER and the next morning, I underwent three emergency thoracic surgeries with an extended stay in the ICU. It was a terrifying experience as my lung had collapsed without any apparent injury, pneumonia, infection, or cause. I later discovered through genetic testing that I have a very rare lung disorder. My life was miraculously spared yet again, and I believe it was for a purpose - to share this truth. At times, I fear that I took my existence for granted, and it took a significant event like this to shake me awake.

The same year proved to be increasingly difficult as my family faced their own life-threatening situations. Life reminded me of its fragility, and each passing day made breathing more challenging. However, I am grateful that I can now feel alive again. Breathing and experiencing life in unique ways has become my quest. It's like waking up to a warm breeze and the sweet melody of birds chirping. Prior to this experience, my heart and soul were already awakening and aware of the purpose for my life, but this event further solidified its shape and significance.

Heartbreak Hotel?

I'd never wanted to be a person to leave others broken-hearted, but somehow, I'd been ok being the person who could be left broken-hearted. I'd made it ok for me to take emotional and mental hits and keep moving. The strong one, the resilient one, became the broken one. My past trauma led me to have a strong desire to help everyone with everything, often neglecting my own soul in the process. However, I reached a point where I made the decision, or perhaps my soul was aching so much that it took control. It wasn't an easy journey, and I didn't do it alone. It took time, prayers, tears, trauma therapy, and vulnerability, but most importantly, I was ready.

In this moment of my life, I have gained enough control to understand the power of letting go and to breathe with confidence. I now realize that it's okay to let things flow like water. Life has a way of delivering gut punches, and people believed I could handle them because I allowed myself to be an emotional punching bag, believing I could handle it. Sometimes, I had to be quiet and focus on myself to truly hear the lessons. It's important to get comfortable with being alone to rebuild oneself, as healing takes time. Embracing silence is also crucial, as it allows us to hear our own directions. It is truly the best gift we can give ourselves.

At the end of each day, we can only change our own behavior and thoughts. It is important to pray for growth and healing for others, as it is a necessary part of our journey. The road ahead may be long and the path may not always be clear, but staying on the course is worth it because we are worth it. The reward that awaits us is intense and fulfilling.

What do you want your world to look like?

Thoughts & Feelings

Date & Time:

Song Choice:

Current Emotion:

<u>Lessons in love</u>

- Appreciate those who surround you.

- You become the 5 people you surround yourself with most often, choose wisely.

- Be kind because it's free.

- Kindness is so simplistically beautiful that it will change your life right before your eyes.

- Stop acting as if you're too busy for the people who care about you. Even the busiest people make time. Time is precious and a currency you can't earn back.

- Pay attention to your self-talk and mindset, negativity knows no boundaries.

- Watch your words, they wield power.

- Protect your energy.

- Heal and give love another try.

- **Treat yourself how you desire to be treated.**

Life is as simple and as beautiful as we allow ourselves to make it. Sometimes we live trapped in the prisons we've created for ourselves out of trauma and fear. Even people who have suffered the greatest heartbreaks and reside in extreme poverty still find reasons to smile. You deserve to smile a true smile. Sometimes we spend so much time making others happy that we miss ourselves. Don't miss yourself! What does fulfillment look like for you? Who would you be if you trusted yourself enough to become that person?

Lastly, I came to understand the profound significance of loving and being loved in a way that resonates with me, in a language that I understand and that feels genuine. I also learned the importance of accepting others and understanding their unique love languages, finding ways to meet them halfway. Additionally, I learned the importance of knowing when to let go of anything or anyone that no longer serves my growth and well-being. Releasing is also an important sign of both love and growth.

Thoughts & Feelings

Date & Time:

Song Choice:

Current Emotion:

Cheers!

Thank you and goodbye to my last year in my third decade, for the valuable lessons you have taught me and the blessings you have bestowed upon me. Hello fabulous forty! I am worthy of wonderful things, and they will come my way. Every day, I will infuse myself with life, love, positivity, compassion, and strength. I will also extend grace, mercy, and patience to myself, knowing that the rest of my journey is still being written. I will not chase after what is not meant for me; instead, I will attract what is meant for me.

I have two favorites that hold a special place in my heart: The fall season and birthdays! Birthdays are incredibly meaningful to me because I have experienced multiple near-death scares. Each birthday I celebrate is a testament to my gratitude for life. I share all of this to emphasize the preciousness of solar return.

Now, let me share a known fact about me—I absolutely adore the fall season! The cozy clothes, warm sweaters, hot cider, vibrant leaves, and the feeling of love in the air make it truly special. Even the scent of the outdoors during fall fills me with joy. Can you relate to this feeling?

Cheers to you entering your thirties, living your thirties and leaving your thirties, it's been a heck of a ride!

Signed,

Becoming Water and Finding Peace

Who am I?

Now Playing:

Brandee Younger- Soul Awakening Kamasi Washington- Becoming Jackie Wilson-Greatest Hits

Anita Baker- Essentials playlist Stevie Wonder- Essentials playlist

I am a friend who loves to plan, the one who motivates and inspires, the person who always wakes up early on vacations and in daily life. I am also the go-to person when it comes to troubles and worries. I understand my role, as we all have our own roles, but I also recognize the importance of being nurtured. Even the strongest friend can get tired, and it's crucial for them to acknowledge that. I've come to realize that it can be challenging for people to nurture a "strong friend", especially when they didn't choose to be strong in the first place. Often, they are forced into this role at a young age. The decisions that are imposed on a child's life can shape them into the adults they become, both in positive and negative ways. Unresolved childhood trauma can lead to breakdowns in all types of relationships. I've gone through many difficult times, but I always manage to come out stronger, just like many others. In my teenage years and early twenties, I often appeared stern, and at times, even cold. It wasn't because I truly was that way, but rather because I was shy and heartbroken and didn't even realize it. There were so many pieces to the puzzle - my parents' divorce, my father starting a new family and my feeling abandoned, navigating the challenges of adolescence without a male role model, and my mom suddenly becoming a single parent. I had to navigate the complexities of dating, while also grappling with the intense emotions and hormonal changes that come with adolescence. In addition, I had endured mistreatment from boys and men lost in their trauma, often disguised as love and care. It was a difficult realization for me, as my understanding of love was shaped by the experiences I had. It felt like an internal struggle, with my soul yearning for a deeper connection while my human form resisted it. This created a profound shock to my nervous system that persisted for a long time. My soul cried out while my human form endured abuse, first from myself and then from others who also only knew the limited human version of love based on their experiences.

Honestly, I simply didn't have a full understanding of what it all meant. Being relational is a complex thing to learn because who really has it all figured out? When my parents were married, there was a lot of teamwork in our household. Both parents cooked, worked, and cleaned. However, I can't say that romantic love was taught to me but acts of service were consistently shown. That became my primary love language, as it was easy to recognize. I have always been a hopeless romantic, but I learned that I desire all of the love languages with physical touch being the primary. I have also noticed that my primary love language changes based on life season and new experiences. I believed that if I did things for others, they would do the same for me but that wasn't their experience with love.

I thought that treating people how I wanted to be treated was the key. Well, let's just say that I had many lessons to learn before I finally found my way to treat myself how I desired to be treated. I never heard my parents argue, not even once. I'm sure they did, but they shielded me from it. Our home was always cool and peaceful, which I am grateful for.

My parents are my best friends and always have been. We would gather as a family to play games, they helped with homework, and we collectively cleaned our home on Saturdays, all while enjoying the soulful tunes of

Motown and the fresh scent of Pine Sol. Our music taste ranged from Jackie Wilson and Anita Baker to even a little yacht rock! On Sundays, we would all attend church, and often our family outings would include a trip to Steak and Ale or Sizzlers. Growing up in New Jersey until I was 12 years old, we would occasionally venture to Bowcraft, Staten Island and Atlantic City on weekends for some occasional fun. Despite facing challenges such as experiencing a few periods without electricity, my parents always found a way to make things okay, and I never felt a sense of panic. These financial difficulties arose from my father's desire to assist others, both within the community and through the church, which unfortunately resulted in unexpected financial losses.

Nevertheless, both my parents did their utmost to cope with these setbacks. They were both generous individuals with kind and compassionate hearts that were impacted by trauma. Sometimes we can lash out at those we love due to those who have taken advantage of us. Proximity and pain. Trauma wins again. Another cycle that made its way around...

As a child, I thought we were simply pretending to camp during those brief times without electricity, but as an adult, I now understand the financial strains we faced. As a parent, I understand the fear of inability. The divorce was the first truly shocking and life-altering event for me, catching me completely off guard. It altered my existence, reshaping everything I would learn and how I would learn it from that point forward. For my parents, like many others, were two individuals with grand love, broken pasts and a limited understanding of love. The heartache and trauma they experienced ultimately devastated their marriage and that cycle continued...

Humanizing my parents

As an adult, I have come to see my parents as more than just my parents; I see them as fellow human beings. Souls having a human experience. This shift in perspective has helped me let go of some of the anger I felt about being caught in the crossfire of their breakup. By humanizing them, I now understand that they were young individuals trying to navigate life while also fulfilling the role of parents. Parenting, I've come to realize, is undeniably one of the toughest jobs in the world, and it's something that people should acknowledge more often when contemplating the journey of parenthood. It presents unique challenges because children have a way of unintentionally exposing our flaws, shortcomings, and triggering our unresolved trauma even when they've done nothing but simply exist. The impact of this realization can range from negative to downright detrimental.

As a man in his mid-20's, I don't think my father fully knew how to navigate that dynamic of fatherhood and marriage. But then again, neither did my mom. They were both just figuring it out as they went along. In a way, we're all just winging it when it comes to adulthood, aren't we? Some days, I felt like I was conquering the world, while other days, I felt like an imposter.

Thoughts & Feelings

Date & Time:

Song Choice:

Current Emotion:

Despite its challenges, my childhood wasn't horrible, which I am grateful for. I always felt loved, based on my own understanding at the time. They never intended to hurt us; it was just a consequence of life happening. A series of unfortunate events ensued. For me, it became a source of success. A certain amount of trauma but not enough that required heavy intervention, was how I made it to the other side. They didn't set out to hurt each other either, but sometimes life can become toxic if we're not careful.

Growing up in our home, there were so many things I loved about my parents. My mom had a distinct scent of "Red Door" perfume and introduced me to the music of Phyllis Hyman and the writings of Terry McMillan, even when she didn't know. These elements taught me about a woman's pain at a very young age. My dad, on the other hand, made the best pancakes and had a subtle cologne called "Pleasures." He also introduced me to the timeless tunes of Motown. These elements tied food and music together for me and still do. Both always dressed impeccably, and I couldn't wait to grow up and dress just like them. I thought they were so elegant and beautiful/handsome. I would often watch my father play the piano with a sense of awe and observe my mother gently applying light makeup to her beautiful face.

I learned many things from my youth. My parents allowed me to be a free thinker and never dimmed my light. I was appropriately disciplined and my goodness, I was a busy body as a kid. They allowed me to just flow and now it feels magnificent! That felt scary once I was a teenager though because they didn't force me into any particular direction. I figured it out eventually and every journey has allowed me new growth in a new season. The military was my first major life decision as an adult, and I felt confident making it. As an adult I learned a lesson from my childhood, that the goal is to create generational wealth, not look rich. That wealth includes emotional, mental, and spiritual wealth for generations to come. Not to mention the necessity for love, compassion, and care amongst one another. You can't buy your way out of a broken heart and the deep sense of loss or into great relationships and lasting bonds.

Parental lessons

Pre-divorce lessons:

My mother has often been referred to as "our Claire Huxtable." She possesses an incredible array of qualities - intelligence, diligence, grace, and beauty. She has a knack for accomplishing tasks efficiently, yet always maintains a gentle touch. Never once did my mother raise her voice or resort to physical discipline with me. I vividly recall the first time I heard her curse, when I was around 11 years old, simply because she had forgotten to buy batteries for the flashlight ahead of an approaching storm. It was a moment of shock for my brother and me, as she had always seemed so perfect. Looking back, I can now laugh at that memory, realizing that none of us are truly perfect, although my parents certainly came close in my eyes. My father taught me that men excel in cooking, cleaning, laundry, child-rearing, assisting with homework, and engaging in conversations that balance both logic and emotion while being scholars. He was also good at most things, swimming, bowling, running, skating and volleyball. Together, my parents taught me the importance of reciprocity in a successful partnership.

Post-divorce lessons

The following lessons were difficult because I am truly a "parents' girl." I have always been extremely close to both parents with an invaluable bond. Their divorce was difficult because of this. Hurt, pain and trauma had altered my parents right before my eyes. My parents were and are the best! At the age of 13, my family relocated to Baltimore, and it was during this time that I began to learn the invaluable lessons of strength and resilience from my mother. However, along with these lessons came the heartache of not knowing when to stop giving and trusting. I hadn't learned when enough was enough. My threshold for emotional and mental abuse had become alarmingly high, a result of collateral damage from the fallout of my parents' divorce. There were moments when it felt like I had caused their pain and that this was my punishment. That without my existence, they wouldn't need to communicate and they would be happier. Kids learn by observing, and unfortunately, I learned to continuously work from a place of sacrifice and exhaustion, which eventually led to resentment and suffering. These were not healthy lessons and unlearning them proved to be a challenging task. However, it is possible to overcome them. These experiences are regrettably common for those who grow up watching a single mother navigate life. On the bright side, it also taught me that I can achieve absolutely anything! It taught me that embracing change opens doors that I should not fear, and that sometimes, I just need to take a leap of faith.

From my father, I unintentionally learned the lesson of not depending on a man. When he moved away and remarried, I experienced a significant loss of time, which taught me that anyone can leave your life whenever they please and that the world doesn't owe you anything. This lesson had a profound impact on shaping who I would become. It marked the beginning of major growing pains. Divorced parents, homelessness, hunger, and exhaustion. I never wanted to rely on a man financially, so I started working at the age of 14 through a youth works program but began babysitting at 13. It felt empowering to earn my own money, but I also realized that it made it challenging for me to recognize when I needed assistance or how to ask for it. Out of fear of not knowing how to handle things if my partner were to leave, I often found it difficult to relax. The fear of becoming complacent or facing financial hardships always loomed over me, and I felt the constant need to have a plan in place and no one had released that burden. This mindset had a dual effect on my relationships. In one phase of my life, I would quickly end a relationship, while in the next phase, I struggled to know when it was time to leave. I would often overextend myself and overcompensate, driven by fear and trauma. I have also been the lost soul who allowed mistreatment in silence, whether it was accepting disrespectful behavior, financially covering things I shouldn't have, staying in relationships past their expiration date, or not valuing my own self-worth. In a way, I was abusing myself. The lack of a clear vision for how I should be treated led to numerous missteps. But we all make mistakes. I just wanted to share a bit about my journey to this current space of self-discovery without telling too much of my parents' story. I remember approaching my 30th birthday, thinking I had finally reached adulthood. What I didn't realize was that I wasn't grown, I was growing…

Thoughts & Feelings

Date & Time:

Song Choice:

Current Emotion:

__The Beginning__

Now Playing- Kanye- Graduation

In this decade, I achieved multiple academic milestones. I earned a second bachelor's degree, obtained my master's in psychology with a concentration in Applied Behavior Analysis, and completed a Post Graduate Certification in Professional Counseling, leading to my Clinical licensure. Interestingly, my adult career began in the Navy. When I finished high school, I had no idea what I wanted to study in college or how I would afford it. My academic performance in high school wasn't the best, not because the material was difficult, but because there was a lack of focus on my success. The divorce of my parents right before I started high school had a significant impact on me. It caused my head and heart to become overwhelmed and distracted. My whole life was turned upside down, and I felt a mix of tension, sadness, and disappointment. I was lost and confused, feeling lonely in a world that seemed so big. I had made many mistakes but never felt like a failure. My mother, as a single parent, had her hands full while taking care of two children. She worked tirelessly, sometimes day and night, to ensure we had food and a place to sleep, even if she didn't get much rest herself. My father wasn't completely absent from my life, but our interactions were limited due to him residing in New York, with only a few visits each year. Truth told, him making more efforts would have positively impacted my dark days and likely minimized them. People can move on from their children due to their pain, a difficult lesson to learn as a child. A teaching moment as an adult and now single mother. My father's absence was so devastatingly impactful because his presence was powerful and loving. Thankfully, with growth, time, accountability, introspection and forgiveness, our relationship has recovered beautifully, and we now have the most healing conversations. High school didn't seem like a top priority for me. I was simply lost in the hustle and bustle of busy city life, where anything could happen every day. It was an adventure, sometimes scary, but occasionally great. Growing up in Baltimore prepared me for the military, and I was unfazed by the yelling and discipline. At the age of 16, I took on two jobs to ease the burden on my mother. Instead of graduating with my peers on the designated date, I had to attend summer school because my interest in it had diminished even further.

My life changed right before graduation on a beautiful sunny day. I was coming out of the school and saw two people approaching in all white. They commanded respect and looked amazing. I wanted that, who were they? They were in the Navy and the recruiter walked right up to me and told me "You need a life outside of here" as if he knew me! He handed me a card and I initially thought "I am not going to the military." He asked me to call him, and I did after a few days. His presentation was top tier. I had decided that I was going to the military because I had no other plan. I had a whole presentation for my parents who were none too thrilled with that decision and were concerned about a war possibly happening and all the things I would have to deal with. I eventually convinced them that it would give me stability and direction, they gave their blessing and so it began. I eventually graduated from summer school, started the DEP program for the military and maintained 2 jobs until I left on January 2, 2001. Best decision of my life! I went to bootcamp in Illinois, in January... bad decision! It was so cold, and the snow was insane! Now New Jersey was snow and ice, and Maryland had its fair share of snow but nothing like the added windchill in Illinois. Boot Camp was pretty cool for me. I didn't mind cutting my hair or waking up early because I have always been an early bird. I made good friends, got in trouble, accomplished different achievements, and did more pushups in one minute than any other time in my life (100 in one minute.) I started my A school in March in Virginia Beach and made some of the best friends that I still have. The military was very much a "good ole boys" club but I went to my ship and had the best ship's crew ever! We were young, messy, funny, and employed! We traveled, laughed, learned, ate some fantastic foods, wasted money, cried from being home sick and comforted one another because we were all we had. Good times and great memories.

Why all the traumas?

Now Playing:

Cadillac Records Soundtrack Beyonce- Trust in Me

All I Could Do Is Cry

I'd Rather Go Blind

Adele- Easy on Me

Chris Stapleton- Tennessee Whiskey Summer Walker- Clear EP

Cleo Sol- Her Light

Have you ever noticed how being in a relationship can sometimes feel like a traumatic experience? It can almost feel like a form of oppression, especially for women. We're bombarded with confusing signals and expectations. We're told to be humble, learn to cook, support our partner's dreams, help pay the bills, keep a clean house, have and raise children, get an education, and have a successful career. On top of all that, we're expected to be attentive and intimate wives, because apparently, it's our responsibility to fulfill our partner's sexual needs. If we don't, we're made to believe that they'll leave us for someone else who will. It's a lot of pressure, and it's no wonder that many women feel disconnected from their own minds and bodies. We're taught from a young age that our purpose is to serve others, while boys aren't really groomed for marriage or given any real preparation. This has created multiple issues which we are still seeing play out in the media today. As a woman, I can only speak from my own perspective, but I'm sure there are men who feel similarly. It's disheartening to see how people are so focused on tearing others down in order to gain something for themselves. Love has been redefined as a transactional experience, where meeting someone's needs is prioritized over everything else. It's an exhausting narrative that needs to be challenged. So what happened in my case, I got married in 2010 and the year is now 2021...

Am I enough?

November 2021

I was always the type of person who prided myself on being focused and composed. I had dreams and aspirations that I wanted to pursue, all while trying to meet the expectations of being a married woman and mom in our society. I wanted to be valuable to my partner. But it turns out, that wasn't enough. I thought I was managing, moving forward, completing tasks, and succeeding. I thought I was simply avoiding trauma, without realizing that I was actually sitting in it. I was functioning on the surface, but internally, I was crumbling. Avoidance became my constant state of existence. Except, in this case, I was competing against myself. I was racing against my own fear of failure. I believed I was fine, until everything hit me all at once. Every thought, every word, everything. It all came crashing down on me simultaneously. All. At. One. Time.

2021 has undoubtedly been one of the toughest years of my life so far. I'm making it through, but it feels like I barely scraped by. It was like being caught in a relentless storm. Despite everything, I somehow managed to juggle a full workload, contribute to half of the household bills, homeschool my children, prepare meals day in and day out, take care of the household, and attend to the mental and emotional needs of my family. On top of that, I made sure to regularly check in with my loved ones, offering them support and love whenever I could. But amidst all of this, I was also hit with a series of rare medical issues, undergoing multiple surgeries, some of which were emergencies And if that wasn't enough, a very close family member was diagnosed with cancer. And placed on top like a cherry… intense relationship turmoil. The challenges seemed never-ending.

Surviving all of this, after experiencing at least three near-death moments, comes with a certain sense of guilt. It made me feel like I needed to be the best at everything because I was given another chance in life. I also felt unworthy, exhausted, pissed and devastated. With time, I remembered that my life is important and that I have a purpose to fulfill. So, I pushed myself even harder, determined not to fail. My entire 15-year relationship revolved around chasing his past, unrealistic expectations, and a constant pressure to be someone or something I wasn't. Me and this family life we created were never going to be enough for him and I had to accept that but couldn't.

*** 2023 update- It's worth mentioning that I don't think he even recognized this situation during those years, and perhaps even now that it's over.

Throughout my life, I have faced my fair share of trauma. One of the most painful experiences I've endured is emotional abuse. I can recognize it as emotional abuse now but saw it as normalized "struggle love" pains that came with some relationships. Such a false narrative that needs to be addressed. It's a peculiar thing because it leaves no physical scars, causing some people to dismiss its significance. But words hold immense power. We should use our words for good, love, education, and support. Unfortunately, many individuals carry unresolved childhood trauma that manifests in damaging ways towards those around them. Emotional abuse can include actions but those actions are not always physical abuse, but can be just as harmful. Yet another cycle... Sometimes we can lash out at those we love due to pain from past trauma. Proximity and pain.

I have always felt the need to overcompensate, which led me to stay in an environment that was hurting me. I did this for years, becoming conditioned to accept certain behaviors if they stayed within my threshold for pain. But once it spilled over, I usually found the strength to respond. However, this time, I couldn't. Sometimes, I found myself remaining in spaces where I wasn't truly loved, despite seeing all the signs telling me to leave. It's as if God sent those signs, yet I stayed. It's a result of conditioning, conditioning, conditioning. But as they say, "you can't heal in the same environment that hurt you."

The Breakdown

I found myself trapped in an environment that caused me pain. Trapped by me, my fears, shame, and exhaustion. I wasn't being true to myself, nor was I honoring my own worth. Unbeknownst to me, I was punishing myself, driven by a deep-seated feeling of unworthiness. Many of the decisions I made regarding relationships with men were rooted in fear and comfort. The fear of being abandoned, so I tried to be everything they wanted. The comfort of the known.

There's always been one thing that terrifies me: the lack of control. As a child, the most significant and life-altering decisions were made for me. It's interesting to reflect on how much those childhood decisions shape our lives, even though they weren't our own choices.

A significant portion of who I became as an adult was a direct result of my watching the women in my family take on more than they could bare. In my case, I found myself operating from a place of abandonment and rejection, and it was evident in my tolerance level.

This past Monday (November 2021), I woke up with a mild headache, feeling generally okay. However, the four days leading up to that had been quite challenging. I experienced sharp chest pains, chest pressure, and arm pain accompanied by a tingling sensation, occurring after 2 am each night. It felt like I was having a heart attack. On the fourth day, I decided to go to the ER, where I was informed that these symptoms were Prinzmetal anginas - a rare form that only occurs at rest. They can be induced by stress or cocaine, but let me be clear, I have never done cocaine.

I didn't feel particularly stressed; in fact, I felt like I was handling everything well, even though I was overworking myself. Sure, I felt a bit overwhelmed, but don't most moms? I did notice my hand shaking while cooking on Sunday morning, but I brushed it off, thinking it was due to too much coffee and not enough water. I hadn't paid much attention to my stomach aches, lack of appetite, lack of sleep, or social withdrawal. I withdrew from social media, convincing myself it was to control what I saw and heard. I distanced myself from people, claiming that I needed to focus on myself for a while. I stopped going grocery and clothes shopping in person, telling myself it was to save money. But, I was trying to find balance instead of addressing and processing my emotions.

I had been hit with something else that was out of my control, but it greatly affected my life based on someone else's feelings. Marital drama with unexpected and inconsiderate behavior led to the emotional explosion. What about me? Why was I never truly considered in the damage that had been done to me? I endured pain in the hopes of finding joy, but all I found was more pain. I felt like I was slowly drowning. I thought I just needed a little space to focus on myself, but at some point, I simply stopped. I never saw it coming - one moment I was okay, and the next, I was consumed by rage. Every pain, every word, every action spewed my way manifested in a physical response in a major way. I was so angry at that moment that I broke everything in front of me. I wanted everything to be as destroyed as I felt. If I could have breathed fire, I would have.

The Great Pretender

I pretended that everything was fine, behaving as if I was strong. Smiling and moving through pain. My smiles were genuine though because I was still grateful for each day. Being seen as strong, I felt the need to keep up that facade. Trauma. I've always been resilient, adaptable most of the time. There were many moments when I wanted to break down, but I couldn't because I had children to raise and responsibilities to fulfill. I believed that if I just continued doing my best, I would eventually have the love and life I deserved. I thought that if I could just endure the trauma and emotional turmoil, I would come out fine on the other side. I was waiting for my partner to go through their own healing process, hoping that it would make them less mean, distant, and unhappy. I internalized all the hurtful things he did and said which shifted me into a sad version of myself.. It seemed acceptable to stay because he wasn't physically abusive, but in the process, I gradually lost myself, my dignity, and my sense of self-worth. I didn't even notice it happening at the time. Trauma.

I started making countless compromises just to keep him around. He seemed regularly unhappy with every aspect of our life for over a decade, and I grew resentful of it. The consistency of his behavior almost broke me. Trauma. Deep down, I knew from the beginning that I was ignoring red flags, like the yelling and cursing at me. But I loved him, all times weren't bad and I believed that with time, the bad would change and I could heal his past wounds and mine. Struggle love. Society often tells women that there aren't many men out there, so we should hold onto the one we have. It's a sad narrative that I bought into it.

Over the years, things only got worse, reaching their peak after the birth of our last daughter. I won't claim to be perfect, because I was failing myself as well. It became increasingly difficult for me to like him, be intimate or connected with a man who spoke to me with such venom. How could I feel loved in that way? There's that cause and effect again. The effects of lack of connection/intimacy stemming from the toxic environment created for over a decade. I didn't talk about it much, but a few family and friends recognized the toxic dynamic. Nevertheless, my loyalty to him, to us, overshadowed any concerns raised by others. I knew it but we both just stayed. Unfortunately, his possible sense of obligation towards me based on my loyalty, coupled with his appearance of unhappiness, likely exacerbated the problems we faced. My childhood issues of rejection and abandonment kept me trapped in broken spaces and made me angry. I don't think he truly noticed how cruel he had become because of his own mental space but I won't speak for him.

If it were so bad, why didn't I just leave? Emotional trauma had become my love language because of my parents divorce causing my mom so much pain that it was projected onto me. My threshold was high and tolerant. If you were to ask him, he probably wouldn't even want to discuss that time in our lives. We have since grown, but not without the destruction of a version of myself and our marriage. I take my blame for not doing the work to heal myself sooner which only exacerbated the situation. I eventually sought heavy trauma therapy through EMDR for PTSD alongside mindfulness based cognitive therapy. Understanding the depths of self was key. When I was almost beaten to death by a man I did not know and sustained a brain injury, I had sustained undiscovered damage. My body damage increased over the years, but memories of it faded with the coma

I was in. Going through trauma therapy gave me the memories back and the freedom from that trauma. Working through past trauma has allowed a fresh perspective on life. Becoming the change I wanted to see. It was an incredibly toxic situation at times but was also my greatest teacher. It wasn't all bad and we even had fun times, laughter, taught one another and had great moments of clarity. We built what we said we would and that matters. There was a time he was my best friend in the world with a cool dynamic. The end was heartbreaking but necessary, I suppose. I won't go into further detail, mainly because we have daughters who may one day read this. He deserves to tell his own story to them. I am sharing my side to provide context for where I am headed next.

Who I've become

Now Playing…

Kindred the Family Soul- I Am

Ebony Jenae- Grateful

Dear Silas- I Aint Stressin' Today

Dear Silas- Thank You

Kirby- Eve Gene

Madison Ryann Ward- Prodigal

Madison Ryann Ward- Higher

Valntna- Glow Queen

Whitney Houston- I'm Every Woman

Avery Sunshine- Safe in His Arms

Savannah Cristina- Confidence

Let's catch up! The day is Oct 11, 2023, and my goodness I have learned a few things. A little more than a year prior to this day, I lost one of my best friends in the world. I'd had him my entire adult life and his death left my soul feeling heavy. We had the same scars from our lung surgeries, similar stories of pain and laughing through how difficult the recoveries were. He was the only person who understood how painful and terrifying it was. His passing shook my world and caused another massive correction from that day on.

This is the day that I realized that I was being bullied for most of my life. This bullying experience involved the act of dimming my light and suppressing my soul. Energy vampires siphoning my energy and diminishing my essence. People often wonder why others don't simply walk away when they feel this way, but the truth is, you don't always realize it. You see, I wasn't just emotionally bullied by other people, but also by my own expectations and notions of who I should be for others, without considering myself. I was suppressing, dimming, and diminishing my own self, which unfortunately taught others that this behavior was acceptable. Hell, their darkness was likely fueling their behavior as well. I have since learned to take nothing personal. As you've read above, my childhood trauma had me in a chokehold. Even in this book you won't learn the full story because I am also a compassionate protector who has learned to release. I am no victim; I have been through victimizing situations but I have come to understand that going through struggles can lead to a successful future, thanks to the power of gratitude.

I started deep meditation, tai chi, intentional breathing and became a certified mindfulness practitioner. I now have stronger boundaries, less tolerance for the unnecessary, improved balance, and a voice that speaks with greater clarity, emotional flow and sound logic. I have emerged on the other side, ready to present this book to all of you. My hope is that one day these books will profoundly impact the lives of many, and that is a gift in and of itself.

Life is built for the lessons and bitterness and resentment will not allow you to learn them. Try not to allow pain to keep you from introspection because you may believe that your pain, your past and trauma should supersede self- accountability.

Everything is temporary.

The gift I would like to leave you with is this: We all play a role in our lives. If we refuse to seek understanding of self and become our best version, we are actively choosing to give up our free will. We have a choice to live the best life we could possibly live with those who provide reciprocal bonds. Remaining in our trauma keeps us from the full light of life. My heart still goes through pains that my eyes reflect when I think of passing down the trauma of a broken family to my daughters. I also rejoice that I have broken barriers to change their lives for the better by the constant work of self healing. The shift in me was learning emotional control, self-care, compassion, empathy, and self-awareness. Black men and women aren't often taught emotional safety or emotional expression, so these waters aren't navigated with ease. Being raised to survive, not thrive, has an impact on the head and heart connection. Trying to comfort and find comfort in two of the most disrespected, oppressed beings on the planet is a difficult feat that has a multitude of psychological implications that have yet to fully be discovered. When you dehumanize a group of people, the group begins to dehumanize and destroy themselves. Long term effects of psychological distress and warfare. Every cultural group of people has their own story, this is just a major part of mine.

The most difficult part of growth, healing and being in my field is understanding why others do what they do. You realize that none of it had anything to do with you. People project what they are. We attract what we are. If we are in pain and anger, we give and attract the likes of that lower vibrational pattern. I do not believe that people want to be cruel, rude, angry, or resentful. I think that the pain becomes darkness, and it makes it difficult to see the light of compassion. You get stuck and that darkness becomes the shield. The badge of honor that protects us from further hurt. Again, survive, not thrive. So much so that the idea of feeling care and compassion triggers rage from anxiety from discomfort. A good example is when feeling uncomfortable with someone showing compassion or care because you may only understand love as pain or chaos, so you create a painful scene to feel love or something to its effect. Once you create it, point a finger, throw rage and the person walks away, you feel relieved and confused. Not quite understanding why but that you had to do it. Those cycles of destruction are from the deep seeded trauma of not feeling good enough to be loved. Or the need to create the toxicity you experienced as love.

The vicious cycle wins again.

How am I able to be this vulnerable? Because this previous version of me no longer exists. While reading through, my heart aches for the younger version of myself depicted in the story. However, due to the internal work I have undertaken, I can truly say that the past is the past. It was not easy until I chose to allow myself to water and flow. It exists as my story but my story is also ever evolving and I choose to turn the pages. I tell this story for others to understand where I came from. Others who may be going through it themselves need a boost of motivation. To see the other side and know that the impossible is possible. That pain leaves you and a brighter life awaits you. Trauma can consume and terrorize you and everyone you love if you don't address it. Please don't allow trauma to win. It seems as if you already realize how valuable and amazing you are because you made it to the end of this book. I hope it has brought you some peace, joy, balance, understanding and solace.

Conclusion

Now playing:

Luther Vandross- So Amazing Anita Baker- Good Love Kem- Heaven

I sincerely thank you from the depths of my soul for joining me on this journey. Thank you for making it to the end of the book. Thank you for your support. Thank you for choosing self-love and healing. I understand that this journey is not easy, which is why I shared mine. On this side of the fence, I am experiencing my greatest love story in all areas of my life and it's beyond amazing. Please don't be afraid to take the leap and release. Many people are trapped in their own minds, which have become prisons.

Without inner work, freedom will never find us. We have a great deal of control over our lives, and I am incredibly proud of you. Sending loving vibrations for the win!

Thoughts & Feelings

Date & Time:

Song Choice:

Current Emotion:

Date & Time:

Song Choice:

Current Emotion:

Made in the USA
Columbia, SC
29 April 2024

34822302R00072